THE EXCLU

CITIZENSHIP

RUTH LISTER

1965-1990

CHILD POVERTY ACTION GROUP

25 YEARS *Working against poverty*

CPAG Ltd, 1-5 Bath Street, London EC1V 9PY

ISBN 0-946744-26-2

The views expressed in this publication are not necessarily those of the Child Poverty Action Group

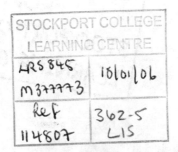

Cover design by Nigel Taylor
Cover photo by Melanie Friend
Typeset by Nancy White
Printed by Calvert's Press, 31-39 Redchurch St, London E2

ACKNOWLEDGEMENTS

The author would like to thank Fran Bennett, Peter Golding, Julia Lewis and Carey Oppenheim for their helpful comments on the first draft; and Valerie Bentley who typed the manuscript. In addition, thanks are due to those who helped with the production of this book, including Richard Kennedy who edited the manuscript, and Nancy White who typeset it.

CONTENTS

CONTENTS

FOREWORD

To be poor is to endure conditional citizenship. This book, which explores the link between poverty and citizenship, launches the Child Poverty Action Group's twenty-fifth anniversary year. Yet after twenty-five years of determined campaigning we clearly have no cause to be jubilant, or even complacent. The growing gap between rich and poor in the Britain of 1990, and the manifest deprivation of countless thousands of families, are salutary reminders that our campaigns must be renewed and invested with even greater energy.

At the heart of this campaigning has been the insistent theme that poverty is not a problem *of* the poor – a sad but inevitable consequence of misfortune, inadequacy, or fecklessness. On the contrary, poverty can only be understood as a feature of society as a whole, disfiguring and diminishing the lives of some as a result of the way we organise our collective way of life.

The right to full and adequately supported membership of the community, of citizenship, has been at the core of CPAG's concerns throughout the Group's history. It is a curious paradox that as we struggle to come to terms with rapid redefinitions of national and cultural boundaries, in Europe and elsewhere, we run the risk of losing sight of the elemental fact that large numbers of people in our own society find their citizenship truncated by virtue of the simple but cruel facts of poverty.

As Ruth Lister so clearly shows, the institutional injuries inflicted by punitive social security regulations, racist and sexist welfare legislation, or increasingly differentiated educational provision, deny large numbers of people their full social rights. As she explains, and as CPAG's earlier book, *Excluding the Poor*, examined in detail, there are major costs imposed by the requirements made by a society increasingly organised around consumption and market values. We are now conceived as customers rather than as citizens. Yet this does not empower us as sovereign consumers so much as it limits our value and our rights to our purchasing power. Where this is grossly unequal so are our rights as citizens. As Conservative MP Sir Ian Gilmour complained, 'under this philosophy everybody is a consumer and the world is a giant supermarket. Life is nothing but a prolonged pursuit of groceries whereby one chooses education from Tesco's and local government from Sainsbury's.'¹ Which is fine for those who can get to Tescos and Sainsburys and can afford to fill their trolleys when they get there.

Ominously, one response to this development has been to see the poor as a group apart. Just as the social explorers of the nineteenth century ventured among the 'ragged' and 'dangerous' classes, so recent writers have begun to cultivate this image of a new 'underclass'. A term coined in post-war America to describe the unemployed urban black population, it resurfaced in the early 1980s, part of a periodic moral panic as a result of which, as one sceptical observer remarks, 'Some extraordinary works of journalism were produced as reporters dipped into the strange world of the truly disenfranchised.'²

For General Booth, observing late nineteenth century London, the denizens of 'Darkest England' were akin to the benighted souls discovered by Stanley in Africa, for 'while brooding over the awful presentation of life as it exists in the vast African forest, it seemed to me only too vivid a picture of many parts of our own land.'³ The new rediscoverers of this 'residuum' come curiously, and tellingly, from widely differing parts of the political spectrum. For Labour MP Frank Field, rising unemployment, widening class differences, growing poverty and punitive public attitudes to the unsuccessful have 'combined to produce an underclass that sits uncomfortably below that group which is referred to as living on a low income'.⁴

For philosopher Anthony Flew, a founder member of the Council of Freedom Association, writing for the right-wing think tank the Social Affairs Unit, the prime need is to focus welfare and relief on the hard core, 'the small minority of the hardship-suffering poor'.⁵ For both writers the new poor of the 'underclass' are a breed apart. Neither would accede to this view so baldly stated, but it is the likely and common endpoint of such apparently differing analyses.

Against this view we have to insist, again and again, that poverty does not make people a group apart from society so much as victims of the injustice and incivilities of the social order of which they are very much a part. It is for this reason that the notion of citizenship is so important. Like the concept 'community', citizenship can be so denuded of precise meaning that it simply offers a comforting warm glow when wrapped around any woolly set of claims or arguments for a vague but better world. Ruth Lister's lucid presentation of the links between citizenship and poverty gives us a firm foundation on which to build the reasoning and campaigns with which to tackle the largest and most damning social problem facing Britain in the last decade of the twentieth century.

Peter Golding

1. *House of Commons Hansard,* vol 124, 17 December 1987, col 1276.
2. M Morris, 'The Poverty Story', *Columbia Journalism Review*, July/August 1987, p48.
3. General William Booth, *In Darkest England and the Way Out*, Salvation Army, 1890,, p11.
4. F Field, *Losing Out: The Making of Britain's Underclass*, Blackwell, 1989, p2.
5. A Flew, *The Philosophy of Poverty: good Samaritans or Procrusteans*, Social Affairs Unit, 1985, p5.

INTRODUCTION

As we enter the 1990s, we can sense a shift away from the narrow, individualistic ethos of the 1980s. An important element in this shift has been the re-emergence of the language of citizenship as a potential challenge to the dominant language of consumerism and enterprise. However, the language of citizenship means different things to different people, since 'the way we define citizenship is intimately linked to the kind of social and political community we want.'[1] Thus the concept of citizenship is emerging as a matter of dispute between the powerful on the one hand and the powerless and those who speak on their behalf on the other.

For the past twenty-five years, the Child Poverty Action Group has been campaigning on behalf of the poor and the powerless. In an article assessing the poverty lobby's role as political defender of the poor, Sarah Benton has suggested that it should 'look to the past for inspiration and return to that longer heritage of ideas about social status and citizenship in which the poor have pressed their demands.'[2]

A twenty-fifth anniversary is an appropriate time for CPAG to reflect on its own past; not as an exercise in nostalgia but as a basis for moving forward. Looking back we find that citizenship was one of the ideals that inspired the Group's early development. Although it did not emerge again as an explicit theme until the mid-1980s, much of CPAG's work can best be understood as a contribution to the wider struggle to extend full and genuine citizenship rights to those excluded by poverty. Unfortunately, it is a struggle that has become increasingly defensive.

The idea of citizenship is an ancient one. In the post-war era, the classic exposition of its meaning was provided by T H Marshall:

> Citizenship is a status bestowed on those who are full members of a community. All who possess the status are equal with respect to the rights and duties with which the status is endowed... societies in which citizenship is a developing institution create an image of an ideal citizenship against which achievement can be measured and towards which aspirations can be directed.[3]

Thus there are a number of dimensions to the concept of citizenship.

At the most fundamental level it is about membership of a community. On a very narrow interpretation, this could be defined on the basis of nationality and citizenship laws. However, given the nature of these laws, this is not an interpretation which we favour since it is essentially discriminatory. Instead, membership of a community is understood in terms of participation in that community. This participation is an expression both of the formal political, legal and social rights and duties of citizenship, and of the social and economic conditions under which they are exercised. That an interaction of the two is critical for the *effective* exercise of the rights and duties of citizenship is one of the central arguments of this book. Finally, citizenship is regarded as an ideal, a goal which is once again acting as an inspiration to those who are trying to construct an alternative vision of society.

The twentieth century marked the extension of citizenship rights from the civil and political to the social spheres. Yet we are in danger of entering the twenty-first century with a growing number of our fellow citizens excluded by poverty from full enjoyment of those rights. It is therefore imperative that the implications of poverty and its various manifestations are central to the current citizenship debate. In campaigning for a fair and just society, it is time to go on the offensive and restate the case for effective citizenship rights for all, regardless of class, race, gender, age, disability or employment status.

The central aim of this book is to make this case, drawing on the work of CPAG over the last twenty-five years. In the process, we also attempt to provide a distillation of the considerable volume of recent material on citizenship. Our main focus is poverty rather than children (whose relationship to citizenship is rather different to that of adults), although Chapter Five contains a brief discussion of children's citizenship rights and the impact of poverty upon them. The same chapter also examines the ways in which women and black people in this country enjoy less than full rights of citizenship.

We begin by looking at the various meanings of citizenship in today's political debate. It is argued that the meaning of citizenship rights and obligations cannot be understood in isolation from the inequalities of power, status and resources (reflecting the dimensions of gender, race and disability as well as social class) that structure them. Thus, the full and effective exercise of legal and political rights requires a firm base of social and economic rights. Part II then examines the way in which the civil, political and social rights of citizenship are still undermined by poverty. We also consider how some of these rights have been eroded in recent years, as the welfare state increasingly turns its back on the citizenship ideal that inspired its architects during and after the Second World War.

The Conclusion looks to the future. It argues that the resurrection of the citizenship principle today could inspire a new generation to build a fairer and more united society. To this end, we propose a charter for social citizenship which goes further than the European Community Charter of Fundamental Social Rights in addressing the social as opposed to the purely economic rights of citizens and in taking on board the crucial question of racism.

PART I

THE CITIZENSHIP DEBATE

1
THE RESPONSIBILITIES OF CITIZENSHIP

Desmond King has argued that 'New Right advocates seek not only to revive the role of market mechanisms and to end collectivist state policy, but also to dismantle the citizenship rights established during the last two centuries'.[1]

Talk of rights is now restricted to the consumer in the market-place, an area in which people with little money are at a distinct disadvantage. The New Right's distaste for *citizens'* rights, and the expectations of the State that they create, permeated the speeches of John Moore when Secretary of State. Most explicitly, in a speech to the 1988 Conservative Party Conference, he set the Party the task of:

> ...correcting the balance of the citizenship equation. In a free society the equation that has 'rights' on one side must have 'responsibilities' on the other... For more than a quarter of a century public focus has been on the citizen's 'rights' and it is now past time to redress the balance.[2]

In redressing the balance, the Right has turned commonly accepted notions of citizenship on their head and exchanged the language of entitlement for that of obligation and responsibility:[3] the obligation of citizenship that must be imposed on the poor to reduce their dependency on the 'benefits culture'; the responsibilities of 'active citizenship' ascribed to those who have benefited from the policies of the last decade; and what has been dubbed 'the new model citizenship' attached to the universal responsibility to pay the poll tax.

(i) The dependent citizen

In an interview in the *Independent* shortly after the 1987 election, the Prime Minister announced her determination to end the 'dependency culture'.[4] This official obsession with dependency echoes the concerns of the New Right in the United States, the source of many of the Government's ideas on social policy. Central to the debate has been Lawrence Mead's thesis that the enforcement of obligations – in particular, work obligations – is 'as much a badge of citizenship as rights.'[5]

Work obligation and workfare

The enforcement of a 'work obligation' is presented by writers like Mead as being in the interests of both the individual poor citizen and the wider society:

> For recipients, work must be viewed, not as an expression of self-interest, but as an obligation owed to society. At the same time, to fulfil this obligation would permit the poor a kind of freedom that benefits alone never can...
>
> An effective welfare must include the recipients in the common obligation of citizens, rather than exclude them...
>
> To require the dependant to function in minimal ways, onerous as it seems, is essential to banish the worst bondage of unequal citizenship...
>
> Given the evenhanded nature of citizenship, only those who bear obligations can truly appropriate their rights.'[6]

There are a number of ways of enforcing a work obligation. One is the US policy known as 'workfare' which involves working or training as a condition of receiving benefit. The UK government has formally rejected workfare and there certainly is a distinction between workfare and restrictive benefit policies which push the unemployed into low-paid work or training. However, the element of obligation is common to both. Examples include the stark choice between YTS (now Youth Training) and destitution which now faces most 16/17-year-olds; and the extension of the period of benefit disqualification for 'voluntary unemployment' (described by the Chair of the Social Security Advisory Committee as 'the English version of workfare'[7]). Similarly, John Moore introduced the second reading of the 1989 Social Security Bill, which tightened up the rules governing entitlement to unemployment benefit, using arguments reminiscent of Mead's:

> Each and every one of these [unfilled job] vacancies is an opportunity for

unemployed people to gain the self-respect and independence that comes from supporting themselves and their families by their own efforts. It is clearly, therefore, the duty of the Government to help them realise that potential, not only for their own sakes but for the good of the country as a whole.[8]

What sort of work?

This is not the place to develop a critique of workfare.[9] Our concern is with the concept of citizenship obligation which underpins both the US scheme and analagous British policies.

As Mead himself makes clear, the obligation to take usually low-paid, often dirty, unpleasant jobs, is central to this debate. Thus it is inaccurate to construe the obligation as providing these prospective new citizens with the same work opportunities enjoyed by more advantaged members of society. Social theorist Bill Jordan has suggested that 'the new orthodoxy's theory of obligation looks like a citizenship-based concept, since the duty is placed on all, and all are supposed to have a common interest in contributing to a productive system from which all benefit. But this is not the case.'[10]

Jordan quotes Mead's observation that 'for both rich and poor alike, work has become increasingly elective.'[11] But the rich can choose to work if it is in their interests to do so, whereas the poor are obliged to work 'because it is in the interests of others (the taxpayers and the rich) that they should do so.'[12]

The key point here is that any 'common interest in contributing to a productive system from which all benefit' is undermined by the fact that the benefits of that system are distributed so unevenly. The development of the rights of social citizenship can be seen as partially neutralising what Marshall termed the 'excessive' inequalities generated by the capitalist system. Far from modifying the inequalities of resources and power generated by the economic system, the social *obligations* of citizenship, as conceived by the New Right, serve to reinforce them.

Dependency and status

Any neutral evaluation of the problem of 'dependency', to which the theory of citizenship obligation is addressed, has to take account of the wider distribution of power and privilege. This was recognised by the Archbishop of York, when he asked how 'if we are to move from a culture of dependency towards a greater degree of responsible freedom, do we strengthen the sense of interdependence between people who differ so markedly in their share of this world's goods?'[13]

Another church commentator has noted that 'power determines whether society regards you as "dependent" or "independent" - dependency is not, in its everyday allocation, a matter of fact but rather a matter of designation'.[14]

Thus, as the Bow Group has pointed out, the dependency of the poor on the visible welfare state of social security benefits is designated very differently from the dependency of the middle class on the invisible fiscal welfare state of tax reliefs.[15]

Marshall placed great emphasis on 'equality of status' in the development of social citizenship. The current preoccupation with the citizenship obligations of welfare 'dependants' accentuates the poor's inequality of status, by defining them as failures.

Obligation and basic income

Proponents of basic income as 'a citizenship-based share of national income'[16] (under which each individual would receive a tax-free payment from the State, regardless of employment or family status) tend to argue that any form of work obligation is incompatible with citizenship. Ralf Dahrendorf has argued this case most explicitly:

> Work involves essentially private contracts, which means that it cannot be traded against citizenship rights... That is not to say that the availability of work is a matter of indifference. People's livelihood, self-respect and even transfer incomes are likely to depend on work for some time to come. But it is to say that citizenship rights and the social contract stipulate unconditional entitlements and that any condition detracts from their quality.[17]

However, some advocates of basic income do accept the necessity for some kind of work condition and that, under a full basic income scheme, with high marginal tax rates, a work test would be inevitable.[18]

Obligation and full employment

It should be stressed that the rejection of a citizenship obligation, as articulated by Mead, does not necessarily imply the total rejection of all forms of obligation. Most citizenship theorists have accepted a place for obligations as well as rights. Thus Marshall maintained that 'if citizenship is invoked in the defence of rights, the corresponding duties of citizenship cannot be ignored.'[19]

More recently, a number of writers on the Left (most notably Raymond Plant), have advocated the principle of work obligation, provided the conditions are right. They point to Sweden, where the obligation to work operates in the context of relatively generous benefits and a commitment to full employment. The latter, of course, was central to the post-war citizenship ideal (for men) but has been sacrificed to the dictates of economic restructuring and the battle against inflation. This retreat from the commitment to full employment by most Western governments since the mid-1970s has fatally eroded 'the prime achievement of social citizenship and the foundation of the welfare state.'[20]

If the appropriate conditions – ie, full employment and adequate regional policies and training programmes – are applied, Plant asks 'what would be wrong with making an able-bodied person's own benefits depend on a stringent availability-for-work-or-training test?'[21]

As noted above, what Plant is talking about is not workfare as such but the kind of availability tests which already apply with increasing stringency. Esam et al, in their proposals for a socialist security system, similarly accept that for unemployed people 'it would have to be a condition of receiving benefit that the individual was willing to work should a suitable job be available.'[22]

If such tests are to be the embodiment of a fair citizenship obligation, then other preconditions are also necessary. In particular, CPAG's longstanding concern with the issue of low pay suggests that they must not merely replace the poverty of the dole with the poverty of low-paid work. This requires a more effective form of minimum wages provision than that provided by the Wages Councils, which set minimum wage levels in a limited number of sectors.

Instead, the Wages Councils are under threat as part of a wider policy that has eroded the citizenship rights of disadvantaged workers. Sheila Allen has argued that 'the abolition of the Fair Wages Clause, the removal of minimum wage protection for young workers and the reduction in wages and health and safety inspectorates seriously undermine the conditions on which working lives are based... Economic or industrial rights as part of a citizen's contract may be argued to be integral to social rights, on which, in turn, the exercise of political and civil rights, for the majority of the population, depend.'[23]

Herein lies the significance of the UK Government's implacable opposition to the recently adopted European Social Charter, which resulted in it being significantly weakened, in particular by the exclusion of any reference to a minimum wage.

Work obligation and women

The notion of obligation is applied rather differently to women than to men, in that a woman's primary obligation is seen as being to her family.[24] However, increasingly the question of a work obligation is also being raised in relation to lone mothers on benefit. In a report for the Social Security Advisory Committee, Joan Brown made clear that 'the lesson from the US is not that workfare or other forms of compulsion are worthy of imitation, but that programmes to induce a return to the labour force have to be focused on the real needs of the individual lone mothers and must be backed by childcare and by other supportive measures.'[25]

Indeed the latter point has been made by Lawrence Mead himself.[26]

(ii) The 'new model' citizen

In the same way that the New Right's theories of dependency underlie the growing emphasis on the work obligation of poor citizens at the expense of their social rights, so their theories of the power of the individual in relation to the State underlie the notion of citizenship obligation implicit in the poll tax. Linking the two is an emphasis on self-reliance. Thus ministers have explained that with regard to local government 'all our policies are designed to give people more control over their own lives' and that:

> ...morality, in this context, includes fairness, but it also encompasses responsibility and self-reliance – the idea that local authorities should be responsible to all of their electors, that every adult should pay his [sic] fair share and play a responsible part in the local democratic process.[27]

Underlying the arguments associated with the poll tax are very different concepts of citizenship. Stewart Miller highlights this point, arguing that the 'new model' citizenship 'emphasises not only social obligations rather than social rights, but also a "progressive" set of political rights which are largely perceived as enabling individuals to protect themselves from the cost implications of expensive communal provision. This inevitably brings this conception of citizenship into conflict with the expansion of social rights on the social democratic model.'[28]

The government thereby justifies the restrictions on local government inherent in the poll tax scheme as a protection of the individual citizen's liberty. However, as Peter Esam and Carey Oppenheim point out in *A Charge on the Community*, 'far from increasing individual power, the poll tax brings with it an army of powers: direct deduction from benefit and earnings, enforcement of joint and several liability and the cohabitation rule, the use of information from personal records, to name just some of them. The poll tax systematically infringes the principles of confidentiality, independence and democracy.'[29]

Moreover, the authors argue that, in reality, it is not the individual citizen's control over local authorities which is being increased, but that of central government.

It is inconceivable that there could ever be a return to the conditional citizenship of the nineteenth century, under which recipients of poor relief were automatically disfranchised (where they otherwise had the vote). Nevertheless, Miller suggests that 'in the new Thatcherite model the same end is to be served by reminding voters – including welfare state clients, who can no longer be separated out so categorically – of the responsibilities and costs of citizenship, expressed in terms of spending impact.'[30]

Miller argues that this linking of political rights to a clear economic framework is as potentially damaging to the social democratic concept of citizenship as is the link between the poll tax and the electoral register (see Part II).

Replacing the concept of the citizen as a member of the community is the idea of 'the new model citizen [who] is essentially a paying customer.'[31] At the same time, at local level at least, a clear link is being forged between democratic participation and taxation. In the words of Nicholas Ridley:

> It makes everyone contribute, at least a little, to local resources, so that all can contribute in democracy at local level.[32]

This is clearly a new twist to the old call for 'no taxation without representation'.

Fran Bennett has pointed out how the notion of the participation of poor people in society has been turned on its head by the rhetoric surrounding the poll tax.[33] The irony is underlined by the language of universalism which is being used to justify the imposition of new obligations on the poor at the same time as it is being expunged from the vocabulary of social security policy. The Bishop of Durham has attacked forcefully the double standards involved:

> It is more and more being made clear that if you are poor and unemployed you are nothing but a burden and a social negativity... To talk about evoking such people's sense of responsibility with regard to their citizenship in a society which treats them like this by, say, making them liable for a proportion of poll tax is ... cruel and insensitive.[34]

(iii) The active citizen

It is, however, the prosperous and successful who the Conservatives regard as the main standard-bearers of citizenship today. According to Joe Rogaly, their patent is 'the "active citizen", an individual who gives money and time to serve the community. This paragon has been invented in response to the argument that the free market, as promoted by Thatcher's government, is hard and uncaring.'[35] Promoted most vigorously by Douglas Hurd, the call to active citizenship is also an attempt to engender social cohesion in the face of growing concern about hooliganism and other forms of anti-social behaviour; to counter the damaging assertion by the Prime Minister that 'there is no such thing as society.'[36]

According to Mr Hurd 'the idea of active citizenship is a necessary complement to that of the enterprise culture. Public service may once have been the duty of an élite, but today it is the responsibility of all who have time or money to spare.'[37]

Thus charitable giving and voluntary service are the two key components of active citizenship. The third element is the denigration of taxation as a means of discharging the obligations of citizenship. This has been a particular theme of John Patten, Minister at the Home Office:

> At one time we were seduced into believing that the most important measure of good citizenship was an uncomplaining willingness to pay high taxes... we have to recognise that it is no longer acceptable to buy your way out of your obligations to society. Tax cannot remain the only way in which citizens discharge their obligations: time and commitment have to be added to money.[38]

Mr Hurd believes that active citizenship 'is a theme which should appeal to people of all parties, and none.'[39] That it does not is a consequence of the particular meaning attached to active citizenship by a government committed to the promotion of private citizenship obligations rather than public rights in an increasingly unequal society. The Government's emphasis on the *duties* of the *active* stands in stark contrast to its neglect of the *rights* of the *citizen*, creating a potential contradiction in terms of the notion in the 'active citizen'.

Despite Mr Hurd's concern that the duty of public service should not be confined to the élite, his notion of active citizenship is inherently inegalitarian. Both he and Mr Patten have directed their exhortations primarily at 'those people doing quite well'; 'the beneficiaries of ten years of unparalleled prosperity'[40] and of successive income tax cuts. Prefiguring the 'active citizen', Mrs Thatcher wrote back in 1977:

> The sense of being self-reliant, of playing a role within the family, of owning one's property, of paying one's way, are all part of the spiritual ballast which maintains responsible citizenship and a solid foundation from which people look around to see what more they can do for others and for themselves.[41]

Thus, lurking behind the active citizen is the successful, self-reliant, enterprising citizen, alias the consuming, property-owning citizen. The unsuccessful and unenterprising are thereby excluded from the ranks of citizens (even though unskilled manual workers give a higher proportion of their incomes to charity than do those in the administrative and managerial classes [42]). Thus, in the name of social cohesion, the Conservative's eulogy to the active citizen merely serves to underline the divisions that exist in our society.

Privatising citizenship

In the name of social cohesion, obligations are also shifted from the public sphere of tax-financed benefits and services to the private sphere of charity and voluntary service. This 'privatised' view of citizenship harks back to the idea of *'noblesse oblige* and moral duty amongst the rich'.[43] The limitations of such an approach were underlined by Andrew Brown of the *Independent,* in an otherwise generally sympathetic account of the Government's position:

> When you hear the Government's rhetoric, the aim seems to be not just to privatise the delivery of welfare, which may be sometimes justified on some grounds of efficiency, but to privatise the obligations involved, which is not charitable … but unjust and iniquitous.[44]

Michael Prowse of the *Financial Times,* noting that 'the Government has so far concentrated on the moral superiority of giving', suggests that 'what it should be asking is what kind of welfare best serves the needs of the unfortunate recipients of aid'.[45] As he and others make clear, the answer is not charity. Reliance on charities simply creates new – or, to be more precise, recreates very old – forms of dependency and passivity. The Bishop of Gloucester, Chair of the Church of England Board for Social Responsibility, has warned that 'to leave the poor dependent on the charity of others threatens their dignity'.[46] From the experience of the United States, Jonathan Kozol writes:

> When rights become gifts, victims cease to be regarded as potential actors on the stage of history and are perceived instead as passive beneficiaries of the actions of the merciful... When charity prevails, food becomes a gift, housing a favour and health care an occasional benefaction. But housing, food and health are not gifts or benefactions. They are the first rights to be claimed by every citizen in civilised societies.[47]

At CPAG's Annual General Meeting in 1988, Sir Ian Gilmour quoted from Michael Ignatieff's *A Just Measure of Pain* which recounted the debates at the turn of the eighteenth century concerning the reform of the Poor Laws:

> Private charity, it was argued, would recreate the face-to-face relationship of dependency and obligation between rich and poor that was sacrificed by a state system. Relief should become a gift of the rich rather than a right to which the poor could lay claim. Pamphleteers were fond of contrasting the poor's insolent clamor at the parish pay table and their 'sparkling eyes, bursting tears and uplifted hands' when visited by Lady Bountiful.[48]

Although these days charity is less often a face-to-face relationship between rich and poor, additional dependencies can be created when assistance is dependent on the intervention of a social worker as intermediary between the applicant and the charity.[49] Indeed, one influential commentator would have us recreate a more direct relationship. In an article lamenting the transformation of charities into campaigning, unionised, bureaucratic organisations, Digby Anderson suggested to readers of the *Sunday Times* that 'we should go out, find the poor ourselves and press a few fivers directly into their hands.'[50] Unfortunately, with more and more people begging on the streets today, this advice is easy to follow.

The other main argument against reliance on charitable giving is that it is unlikely to result in an efficient or fair allocation of resources in relation to need. This is confirmed by Robert Morley, Director of the Family Welfare Association:

> Charity trustees see a moral objection to the basic needs of very many poor people ... being met by the charity and generosity of a few. By its nature, charitable giving is capricious, often spontaneous and rarely the object of careful thought about the needs of poor people and how those needs ought to be met.[51]

Similarly, the Archbishop of York has warned that appeals to individual generosity should not be 'at the cost of those whose needs are unfashionable or unnoticed'.[52]

The growing reliance of social security claimants on charity to meet their basic needs pre-dated the birth of the active citizen.

During the 1980s, CPAG and other organisations documented the impact of successive cutbacks in single payments and their eventual replacement by (primarily) loans from the cash-limited social fund.[53] Increasingly, the charities are reporting that they simply do not have the funds to cope.[54]

In a 1989 *Poverty* editorial, Fran Bennett argued that charity, like means-tested benefits, has never been able to prevent poverty; it serves only to pick up the pieces.[55] Twenty-three years earlier, a similar point was made in the very first edition of *Poverty*. In a comment on a letter from a family describing what Christmas would mean on a low income, it maintained that 'the problem is too big to be solved by private charity alone – and anyway, the Clarkes do not want charity, whether private or public. What they want is a decent income which will be theirs by right.'[56]

Part of the challenge that has always faced groups like CPAG has been how the generous, charitable impulse that is tapped by individual stories of hardship can be translated into support for redistributive tax-benefit policies. This requires not an appeal to charity but to justice. This point has been made forcefully by the religious affairs editor of the *Sunday Correspondent*:

> One of the great fallacies of individualism in the Church has been the idea that social evils can be rectified by philanthropism. Where evils in society are structural, the act of increasing donations to charity offers palliatives rather than solutions... A new sense of social responsibility is, as Mrs Thatcher perceives, essential. But it must not simply drain the superfluity of the young's new prosperity. It must offer the insight that the first principle of true charity is to offer justice. Where injustice lies in structures, so must the solution.[57]

A survey carried out for the Charities Aid Foundation suggests that the great majority of people in this country believes that it is the role of government, not charity, to provide for those who cannot care for themselves. The Foundation's director, Michael Brophy, has made clear that 'if the Government wants greater levels of giving and commitment, it has to do more than just call for "active citizenship". As a minimum, it has to maintain its own spending and make its own role and responsibilities clearer.'[58]

Privatising activity

The same argument applies with regard to active citizenship in the guise of voluntary work, where inevitably there are fears that active citizens will be used to plug the gaps in the statutory services. The extent to which these gaps are already plugged by the invisible work of women – whose caring work in the home does not seem to qualify them for active citizenship medals – also needs to be made clearer.[59]

Another group of active citizens who tend to be overlooked are those poor people who, far from sunk into a state of passive dependence, are 'active in the inner cities and peripheral housing estates'. Pointing to the multiplicity of credit unions, play schemes, tenants associations, welfare rights groups and so forth on the estate where he lives and works, Bob Holman has observed that 'active citizenship certainly has not declined here in the days of the welfare state'.[60] Yet, although Douglas Hurd insists that 'we are committed to encouraging active and responsible citizenship in people of all ages and from all sections of society',[61] it seems clear that the government regards the poor as the objects, not the subjects, of active citizenship. There is a tacit understanding that while the philanthropy of the middle classes is the hallmark of active citizenship, the campaigning of welfare rights groups and the like constitutes the undesirable face of political activism. It is no coincidence that Government reference to self-help groups tends to be predominantly concerned with middle-class activities such as Neighbourhood Watch Schemes.

This top-down notion of citizenship has attracted most criticism from those sections of the Left associated with Charter 88. *New Statesman and Society* has argued that 'citizenship is no more likely to trickle down from the top than wealth. It has to grow up from the bottom.'[62]

Anthony Barnett has been particularly scathing. In an article attacking the idea of a youth volunteer force promoted by the Speaker's Commission on Citizenship and the Prince's Trust, he argued that 'active citizenship is not simply an evasion of the undemocratic realities of Britain today, it is a provocation; an attempt to seize the initiative on citizenship so that citizenship can burn.'[63]

It is possible to share Barnett's anger at the hijacking of the concept of citizenship without necessarily rejecting initiatives such as those proposed by the Speaker's Commission. David Blunkett, who sits on the Commission, has argued that such schemes should be welcomed as an expression of communitarian values, challenging those of individual self-interest which have dominated Government policy. But the limits of such proposals have to be understood:

> Government makes the policies: the active citizens take over bandaging the casualties... The activity of the active citizens is to pick up the victims of the free market and the swimming survivors of the sunken welfare state.'[64]

In one of many ruminations on the active citizen, Douglas Hurd suggested that government 'can remove some of the impediments to human endeavour. It can help set the tone – the public ethos – within which we conduct our daily lives.'[65] However, this government has to take responsibility for having promoted an ethos founded on narrow, competitive individualism in which success is rewarded and failure penalised. The magic wand of active citizenship will not conjure away the consequent widening of social divisions nor create social cohesion where none exists. The latter requires citizenship policies designed to counteract these divisions, not citizenship policies which encourage them.

Conclusion

Citizenship has been redefined on the Right using the language of obligation and responsibility. Three variants have been discussed in this chapter. First is the work obligation imposed upon the poor as a means of combating the 'dependency culture'. In practice this tends to operate as an obligation to take low-paid, unpleasant jobs, thereby reinforcing existing labour market divisions.

Second are the 'new model' citizens who, in the name of self-reliance and accountability, will be paying their 'fair share' for local services through the flat-rate community charge. A link is being forged in the mind of the local electorate between the level of poll tax tax paid and the exercise of the citizens' right to vote, effectively tethering the exercise of citizenship rights to a clear economic framework. At the same time, the language of universality, jettisoned from social security policy, is invoked to justify the imposition of the poll tax on (virtually) everyone, however poor.

Third, the new model citizen is also the active citizen. Charitable giving and voluntary activity are now the hallmarks of good citizenship. In this way, obligation is shifted from the regulated public arena of tax-funded benefits and services to the uncertain private arena of good works, and the beneficiaries of a decade of redistributive policies to the better-off are made to feel good.

In each case the emphasis on the obligations of citizenship serves to obscure and reinforce the inequalities of power, resources and status that an earlier emphasis on the rights of citizenship sought to combat. If the enforcement of the obligations of citizenship is to be just, it must be based on a recognition and strengthening of the rights of citizenship.

2
THE RIGHTS
OF CITIZENSHIP

As we have seen, the Right's project during the 1980s was to undermine the post-war concept of citizenship as rights and the expectations of the State founded on such a conception. Citizenship has been redefined in the language of obligation and the active citizen has been summoned like the Genie of the Lamp to apply a caring gloss to the assault on social and economic rights.

At the same time, sections of Britain's Centre and Left have found a new inspiration in the old notion of citizenship as the basis of rights in the social and economic as well as the civil and political spheres. For some, this rediscovery represents the elusive 'big idea' needed to shape an alternative vision to that offered by Thatcherism.[1] As such, it represents both a reaction to the governing ideology of the past decade and an ideal to win support for a very different set of values for the coming decade.

Citizenship rediscovered

The new appeal to citizenship is a reaction against the arid tenets of market liberalism; its worship of enterprise and consumerism; its narrow conception of freedom; its retreat from collective welfare and the consequent widening of social divisions. As Ralf Dahrendorf has observed 'the decade of wild, often thoughtless, always greedy, growth has, in fact, raised the issue of citizenship for all anew'.[2] According to the *New Statesman and Society,* which has been instrumental in reviving citizenship as a rallying call for those to the left of the present Government, 'it provides grounds for a critique both of the undemocratic British state ... and of regressive social policies'.[3]

As a positive force, the *New Statesman and Society* argues that citizenship 'also offers the best hopes of reconciling individualism and social justice'.[4]   This theme is echoed and amplified by Stuart Hall and David Held:

Citizenship rights are *entitlements*. Such entitlements are public and social... However, though citizenship is a social status, its rights are entitlements to individuals... The 'politics of citizenship' today must come to terms with, and attempt to strike a new balance between, the individual and the social dimensions of citizenship rights. These two aspects are interdependent and cannot be separated.[5]

This balance is central to the work of CPAG which has always fought for the social rights of individual citizens.

The main focus of the *New Statesman and Society*'s project for citizenship, translated into Charter 88, has been the civil and political rights necessary to turn subjects into citizens: 'political and social beings with a role to play in society'.[6] Together with genuine democratic rights, the emphasis is on a bottom-up notion of power and on citizenship in its 'active mode' of political participation, not to be confused with Mr Hurd's 'active citizen'.[7]

These elements of citizenship are, of course, important but, if they are to 'reconcile individualism to social justice' they have to be integrated with the social dimension of citizenship. As J M Barbalet has written:

The issue of who can practice citizenship and on what terms is not only a matter of the legal scope of citizenship and the formal nature of the rights entailed in it. It is also a matter of the non-political capacities of citizens which derive from the social resources they command and to which they have access. A political system of equal citizenship is, in reality, less than equal if it is part of a society divided by unequal conditions.[8]

The notion of social citizenship is at the heart of any consideration of the relationship between citizenship and poverty; we will explore its meaning in Part II. Here our concern is simply to look at how ideas about social citizenship have been resurrected in recent years by members of the Centre and Left. Broadly speaking, we can identify two developments in thinking about social citizenship. The first, more mainstream, approach is that identified with authors such as Ralf Dahrendorf, Frank Field, Charles Murray and Paddy Ashdown; writers whose work is presented primarily as a response to the development of a so-called underclass. The second approach can be loosely associated with contributors to *Critical Social Policy* and

Marxism Today; work which is distinguished by its focus on the need for citizenship theory to acknowledge the challenges posed by feminism and anti-racism. It also attempts to link citizenship rights to considerations of human need and democratic accountability. These two approaches are not necessarily mutually exclusive nor do they represent all that is being written about social citizenship today.[9] However, together they encompass key issues in contemporary writings about the rights of social citizenship.

The perils of the 'underclass'

In 1987, the *New Statesman* published an essay by Dahrendorf, in which he maintained that 'the existence of an underclass casts doubt on the social contract itself. It means that citizenship has become an exclusive rather than an inclusive status. Some are full citizens, some are not.'[10]

This argument aroused some media interest, notably an edition of 'Weekend World' which painted a lurid picture of life in the 'underclass'. The theme was then taken up by Paddy Ashdown in *Citizens' Britain* and by Frank Field MP in *Losing Out.* The main thesis of the latter is that 'the 300-year evolution of citizenship as an incorporating force in British society has been thrown into reverse' and that it 'is the loss of a comprehensive approach to citizenship that makes it appropriate to talk in terms of an emerging underclass'. Four main 'forces of expulsion' – unemployment, widening class differences, the exclusion of the very poorest from rapidly rising living standards, and a hardening of public attitudes – have created 'the underclass' which has become separated from the rest of society 'in terms of income, life chances and political aspirations'.[11]

What is more contentious is the use of the 'underclass' label to describe those so excluded. This is not the place to develop a full-scale critique of the concept of the 'underclass'.[12] However, it has to be said that the use of a concept so imprecise, emotive and value-laden could serve simply to weaken further the poor's claims to citizenship in the eyes of the rest of society, even though this approach is effective as a means of putting poverty in the headlines.

As John Macnicol has argued, and right-wing American writer Charles Murray accepts, the 'underclass' label is simply the latest of many which have been stamped on certain groups of people who are poor, who are delineated primarily by moral rather than economic characteristics.[13] Such definitions do not lend themselves easily to statistical analysis. Murray concedes that it is a waste of time trying to count the 'underclass' as 'it all depends on how one defines its membership... The size of the underclass can be made to look huge or insignificant, depending on what one wants the answer to be.' (Not that this stops many people from trying to quantify the 'underclass' with estimates ranging from 5 to 30 per cent of the population.)[14]

'Underclass is an ugly word,' writes Murray; but so too is the language of many who write about it. For example, Murray described himself as 'a visitor from a plague area come to see whether the disease is spreading'.[15] Dahrendorf described the 'underclass' as 'a cancer which eats away at the texture of societies' and its future development as 'critical for the moral hygiene of British society'.[16]

Frank Field is careful not to use such language and is aware of the dangers of such a victim-blaming approach. His work explicitly focuses on the forces that are excluding poor people from the wider society, rather than the characteristics of the poor themselves. Nevertheless, the very imprecision of his own definition of the 'underclass' leaves his work open to appropriation by those who do not share his concerns.

The language of disease and contamination conveys a pathological image of people in poverty. The *Sunday Times*, in an editorial to mark its publication of Charles Murray's exposé of the British 'underclass', stated that:

> ...it is characterised by drugs, casual violence, petty crime, illegitimate children, homelessness, work avoidance and contempt for conventional values... The underclass spawns illegitimate children without a care for tomorrow and feeds on a crime rate which rivals the United States in property offences.[17]

The danger is that the more that certain groups in poverty are described in such value-laden language, the easier it becomes for the rest of society to write them off as beyond the bonds of common citizenship. And because of the imprecision of the underclass-label and the indiscriminate manner in which it is applied by the media to describe the poor in general, the danger is that this wider group of poor people will be similarly written off.[18]

Yet little tangible evidence has been presented to support the thesis that there is an 'underclass' of poor people who reject the values and aspirations of society at large. That there have always been some groups of people who fit this description is not the point. Indeed, one of the most noteworthy aspects of Murray's article for the *Sunday Times* was that the people interviewed by the paper's reporter did not, in fact, display the characteristics attributed to the 'underclass'.

A recent study of families on benefit by Tyneside CPAG concluded that 'at a time when British poverty is again being discussed in terms of an underclass, it is of crucial importance to recognise that these families, and probably millions more like them living on social security benefits, are in no sense a detached and isolated group cut off from the rest of society. They are just the same people as the rest of our population, with the same culture and aspirations, but with simply too little money to be able to share in the activities and possessions of everyday life with the rest of the population.'[19]

David Harris has argued that social policies which incorporate citizenship principles 'are those which protect the status of beneficiaries as full members of the community by defending them against stigma and guaranteeing, on legitimate terms, access to a community way of life'.[20]

Those who invoke the development of an 'underclass' to make the case for the restoration of full citizenship rights to the poor are playing with fire. They are using a stigmatising label to make the case for non-stigmatising policies. At the same time, the Right is arguing that part of the answer to dealing with the development of an 'underclass' lies in the revival of social stigma: 'Social stigma is an essential ingredient of social order and must, slowly and cumulatively, be restored.'[21] Overall, the policy lessons drawn from Murray's 'underclass' thesis combine a counsel of despair – since central Government is 'powerless' to intervene – with calls for tougher social control and law and order policies. The effect, as Kenneth Thompson warned in the *Sunday Times*, 'could be to denigrate the struggles of the poor and the efforts of those who work with them, whilst giving comfort to those who wish to whip up "moral panics" and cut back on social spending.'[22]

Radicalising citizenship

Some of the earlier uses of the term 'underclass' in both the United States and Britain referred specifically to a racial phenomenon. Although, today, Field makes little mention of the exclusion of black and other ethnic minority groups, Dahrendorf emphasises that the 'underclass' is 'also a phenomenon of race, both in the US and in Britain'.[23]

The issue of race – together with that of gender – is central to some recent writings on the Left which have been critical of traditional liberal conceptions of citizenship. Stuart Hall and David Held contend that what liberal theory has taken for granted has to be contested:

> Namely, whether the existing relations between men and women, between employers and employees, between the social classes or blacks, whites and other ethnic groups, allow citizenship to become a reality in practice.[24]

Fiona Williams has similarly argued that this question is central to the development of a more critical social policy and she suggests that feminist and emerging anti-racist critiques of the welfare state 'have challenged the notion of citizenship by demanding full political and civil rights to all, regardless of sex, ethnic origin or immigrant status'.[25]

The theme is further developed in a recent special Citizenship edition of *Critical Social Policy*. Here, the liberal conception of citizenship, which underpinned the development of the welfare state, is criticised for 'ignoring both the patriarchal and racist structures of state welfare which separate and disunify "universal" interests and for its eurocentric and nationalist understanding of citizenship'. In both cases, the reality of power relations is overlooked. 'The liberal history of citizenship', it concludes, 'must be viewed in the context of a set of *inclusionary* and *exclusionary* practices, aimed at consolidating a particular set of social relations and of rights and entitlements.'[26] The extent to which women and black people have always been the victims of exclusionary practices is all too often ignored by those who deplore today's retreat from supposedly universal citizenship rights.

Two other themes which run through the *Critical Social Policy* contributions and other contemporary writings on citizenship are the relationship between rights and needs, and the importance of democratic participation.

The former is essentially a restatement of the case for effective rights of social citizenship to underpin formal civil and political rights, but based on the development of a theory of human need.[27] The latter incorporates two main strands. One is the case made by writers like Suzie Croft and Peter Beresford for enabling poor people to have a voice:

> Since a crucial starting point of critical debates is the poverty of most people's citizenship, it seems important not to reinforce this by excluding them from the discussions.[28]

The other, which has also been developed by Croft and Beresford, is that of 'user-involvement' in, and the democratic accountability of, welfare institutions. Versions of this alternative conception of 'active citizenship' have been emphasised by Ignatieff and Plant and by the authors of a recent attempt to develop an alternative social and economic policy agenda for the Left (the Sheffield Group); the latter argues for a dual strategy based on concepts of citizenship and democracy, 'embracing top-down centralised rights and bottom-up decentralised initiatives'.[29] Some of these issues are explored further in Part II.

Conclusion

Citizenship has been resurrected among sections of the Centre and Left in reaction to the values of the market-place and as an ideal which helps to reconcile the demands of individualism and social justice. One strand has been a politicised version of the active citizen, where the emphasis is on political and civil rights. Another has highlighted the exclusion from full social citizenship of a growing 'underclass'. It has been argued here, however, that the use of a stigmatising, imprecise and value-laden concept such as 'underclass' could serve to undermine further the citizenship claims of poor people. A third strand has been an attempt to radicalise the concept of citizenship by incorporating into it questions of race and gender and by relating it to notions of human need and democratic accountability.

PART II

CITIZENSHIP
AND
POVERTY

INTRODUCTION

A number of points emerge from our review of the current citizenship debate which provide a framework for a discussion of the relevance of the citizenship ideal for the long-standing concerns of CPAG.

First is the interdependence of the three elements of citizenship identified by Marshall: the civil, the political and the social. In particular, the effective exercise of civil and political rights is partly dependent on an effective floor of social and economic rights.[1] As Brian S Turner has noted: 'Citizenship may be defined in various ways (by reference to civil, legal and social features) but citizenship rights are essentially concerned with the nature of social participation of persons within the community as fully recognised legal members.'[2]

Second, a traditional preoccupation with the relationship between citizenship and social class has served to obscure ways in which citizenship participation has been limited by other important determinants of social position, such as gender, race and disability.

Third, underlying both the above, is the fundamental point that our understanding of citizenship rights and obligations cannot be divorced from their wider social and economic context and the inequalities of power, resources and status that permeate it.

Part II now explores these themes in relation to the work of CPAG over the past twenty-five years. The main focus will be social citizenship, following a brief look at the ways in which inadequate rights of social citizenship have undermined, and continue to undermine, civil and political rights.

3
THE CIVIL ELEMENT

*The civil element is composed of the rights necessary for individual
freedom ... and the right to justice. The last is of a different
order from the others, because it is the right to defend and assert
all one's rights on terms of equality with others and by due
process of law.* [1]
                                                            David Harris

The inability of many poor citizens to assert their 'rights on terms of
equality with others and by due proces of law' was a central theme of
CPAG's work in the late 1960s. *Unequal Rights*, the very first
pamphlet the Group published in 1968, in conjunction with the
London Cooperative Education Department, reproduced the
speeches given at a conference on the legal rights of poor people the
previous year.

The importance of a clear entitlement to welfare and of access to
legal services as rights of citizenship was a recurrent refrain (see also
page 63). In a foreword, Tony Lynes, CPAG's first Secretary/
Director, noted that the conference marked an important stage in the
work of the Group. He underlined the link between rights, living
standards and society's attitudes towards poor people, in terms
highly relevant to the 'underclass' debate:

> So long as we treat large numbers of our fellow citizens as paupers we shall
> continue to *think* of them as paupers, for whom a bare subsistence is
> enough. Only when we stop treating them as an alien 'them' and accord
> them full rights as equal citizens of a responsible society – only then shall
> we be ready to revolt against the inadequacy of the standards of living to
> which so many families are now condemned.[2]

The following year, the first *Poverty* pamphlet, *A Policy to
Establish the Legal Rights of Low-Income Families,* heralded a number

of papers which developed the case for measures to provide proper access for poor people both to the formal legal system and to the system of administrative law, in particular, welfare tribunals.

These early publications dealt with issues such as the inadequacies of the legal aid and advice scheme; the need for a network of legal and advice services; the importance of rights to welfare backed up with adequate information; and, the potential for using the courts to extend poor people's rights. A *Poverty* editorial, looking back over CPAG's first four years, commented:

> Publicity about benefits, pressure on central and local authorities to administer services and benefits in a more rational and dignified way, encouragement and assistance in the use of appeal machinery - these have all been ways of asserting the right to equal citizenship as well as an adequate income. The setting-up of a CPAG Legal Department at the beginning of this year was the natural culmination of these activities.[3]

It is striking the extent to which the citizenship ideal provided the rationale for the development of this second strand to CPAG's work, reflected in the establishment of the Citizens' Rights Office in 1970. 'The Citizens' Rights Office has thus become known as an organisation concerned with the welfare rights of the citizen,' wrote the Group's director Frank Field in 1972.[4] Looking back over this period, Tony Prosser commented, in his study of the Group's test case strategy, that 'a growing stress was placed on the need for an improvement in legal services for the poor as a necessary element in enabling them to achieve full citizenship.'[5]

The attempt to use the law to extend the rights of social security claimants was inspired, in part, by the United States. However, in an early CAPG publication, Hilary Rose warned of the difficulties of translating the American strategy to the British context:

> In the American welfare rights experience, it has been particularly meaningful to resort to law, since the manifest goals of the free and democratic society which are not enshrined within the Constitution are not only frequently more attractive than the actual practice of citizenship rights, but are as law well-honed weapons to define and extend citizenship in practice. It is difficult to see British Law, in its combination of precedent and obscurity, fulfilling the same sort of role.[6]

Tony Prosser concluded that early hopes that the courts could be a useful vehicle for social change were disappointed.* Nevertheless, he argued that this did not devalue the importance of CPAG's legal work, which had been important in the diffusion of welfare rights skills and resources through other groups and the wider community.

Welfare rights

Again, CPAG's development as a welfare rights organisation as well as a lobbying agency was initially influenced by the welfare rights movement in the US. Indeed, in 1987 a *Poverty* editorial asked whether there was not a need for a similar movement in the UK which would allow 'some at least of the materially and socially deprived groups in our society ... [to] themselves assert their fundamental human rights to equal citizenship'. However, in the event the establishment of the Citizens' Rights Office (and the subsequent development of both independent and local authority-based welfare rights agencies) marked the beginning of the professionalisation of welfare rights work rather than the birth of a movement. Nevertheless, CPAG was clear from the outset that welfare rights work was not simply about securing the rights of individual poor citizens within the present system, but also about extending those rights. In another early CPAG pamphlet, Rosalind Brook emphasised that 'in a strategy for rights, we must be clear in our objectives. We need to expose the inadequacies of the welfare state and to demand the right to more and better information... We should seek to eliminate the arbitrary and biased procedures which are within the social services, for example, particularly housing, welfare and social security... A strategy for equality should be concerned with rights.'[8]

The next two decades saw a continuance of this dual emphasis on welfare rights, both as a mechanism for securing the rights of individual citizens and as a challenge to the inadequacy of those rights. However, the very complexity of the social security system has worked against such endeavour. Although a citizens' welfare rights

---

*However, the success in the Jackie Drake case which extended invalid care allowance to married and cohabiting women indicated the European courts might prove a more fruitful future focus for a test case strategy.

movement never materialised, Pete Alcock has nevertheless suggested that welfare rights work can be 'empowering and participative, not paternalistic and professional, like other welfare services'. This is a theme which also runs through the recent report of the Central Council for the Education and Training of Social Workers on welfare rights training in social work education. In a perhaps unduly optimistic article on welfare rights and citizenship, Alcock argues that welfare rights 'provides the basis for an appeal, for a new approach to the delivery of services throughout the whole of state welfare. And linked to the concept of citizenship, as the individual basis for a rights approach to welfare, it provides a manifesto for campaigning for state welfare for all... Most of the advantages of citizenship are, at present, being conducted largely in academic terms; in welfare rights work they can be seen to have an already existing practical reality.'[9]

Social security tribunals

One important potential avenue has been the social security tribunal system. In the first of a number of CPAG pamphlets on the appeals process, R J Coleman emphasised that 'in disputes between public authorities and the citizen, English law has attached considerable importance to the right to a hearing by a more or less independent tribunal.'*[10] However, the experience of the Citizens' Rights Office demonstrated the difficulties some claimants faced in exercising this right. This prompted two further studies of the tribunal system which cast doubts on the assumption, articulated (critically) by Kathleen Bell: 'that the citizen would, through such machinery, be able to exercise his [sic] rights more effectively'.[11]

Bell emphasises the role of the tribunal system, both as a guarantor of citizens' rights to 'welfare property' in the same way that the courts protected rights to more conventional property and as a vehicle for citizen participation:

> Citizenship of the welfare state must embrace more than the right to the traditional role of passive receiver of state services. It must provide

---

*That important right has, of course, now been removed with respect to the social fund.

opportunities for people to become more actively and responsibly involved in the business. In other words, we are looking for a 'better fit' between people's roles as claimants and as citizens of the welfare state... We need to build institutions which foster civic competence, personal responsibility and active involvement... Tribunals should be that kind of institution.

However, her own research indicated that many appellants 'were left with a feeling that they had failed to carry the business through satisfactorily, and this did not add to their self-image as mature and competent citizens of a democratic welfare state.'[12]

Despite considerable improvements in the tribunal system, thanks in part to the research undertaken by Kathleen Bell and CPAG, a recent study into why appellants fail to attend tribunal hearings suggests that Bell's gloomy conclusion still holds today. Author Matthew Farrelly suggests that 'contrary to viewing their appellant experience as participation in the exercise of their democratic rights, as an expression of their citizenship, people ... viewed their experience as one of intimidation, alienation and powerlessness.'[13]

Ninety-eight per cent of those interviewed for Farrelly's study did not even understand the appeal papers clearly, a problem which was particularly acute for those for whom English was not their first language. A survey by the Adult Literacy and Basic Skills Unit found that over a third of those whose first language was *not* English could read English little or not at all; fifty-five per cent wanted to improve their English so that they could understand their rights as British citizens.[14] The failure of the tribunal system to take any real account of the needs of this group is condemned by Farrelly as evidence of institutionalised racism which is undermining citizenship rights.

Farrelly's general conclusion was that an expansion of advice and advocacy services is essential if all tribunal appellants are to be able to make effective use of their rights. This echoes the recommendation of the Social Services Select Committee that 'resources be made available to make it possible for all claimants to be represented at tribunal hearings.'[15] The statistics have shown consistently that representation and attendance at social security tribunals are crucial to success.

Legal aid, advice and information

The need for a national network of advice and information services and for adequate facilities for tribunal representation was an important theme in CPAG's early work. The Group also campaigned for the extension of legal aid to social security tribunals. In a 1970 memorandum to the Lord Chancellor's Advisory Committee on Legal Aid and Advice, Frank Field referred back to the Group's 1969 policy statement on legal rights:

> It is a measure of the lack of progress towards a legal system which, in Professor Titmuss's phrase, helps the poor to protect their badge of citizenship, that we do not have to amend [the earlier criticism of the absence of legal aid for tribunals].[16]

That sixteen years later the Council of Tribunals was still making the case for the (partial) extension of legal aid to tribunals is an even more sobering measure of lack of progress in this area.[17]

More generally, the legal aid scheme has always been recognised as crucial in providing access to the law for people with limited means. Marshall himself discussed the Bill that introduced the scheme in his essay on citizenship and argued for either a universal or almost universal system. A call for a reappraisal of the legal aid means test was made by Martin Partington in a 1978 CPAG pamphlet[18] which contended that the problems associated with the level and operation of the means test too often acted as a barrier to the poor. With the advent of the Legal Action Group, CPAG has paid less attention to questions specifically concerned with legal services issues. Nevertheless, the problems have not gone away and recently renewed concern has been expressed about the legal aid means test and the access of poor people to legal services.

A report last year by Cyril Glasser, a former consultant to the Lord Chancellor's Advisory Committee and contributor to the early work of CPAG, demonstrated that between ten and thirteen million people had dropped out of the legal aid net over the previous decade; it predicted that within two years fewer than forty per cent of the population would qualify for legal aid and only a fifth of families with children – half the proportion eligible nine years earlier – would do so.[19] The recent announcement of a £5 million legal aid package together with a wide-ranging review of the financial conditions for legal aid has gone some way to meet these concerns. However, even the Law Society, while welcoming the package, pointed to its modesty in the face of the number of people who have fallen out of the legal aid net over the past decade.

Although it is not the poorest who are excluded by the legal aid means test, a mixture of underfunding and the new Legal Aid Act have prompted other fears about the erosion of the service provided through the legal aid scheme. A former Chair of the Legal Aid Practitioners Group was quoted in the *Guardian* as warning that the legal aid system provides 'a fundamental bulwark of liberty and justice, yet it is being gradually dismantled without anyone noticing. The number of access points has been reduced, the quality of service has been reduced, and people are made to wait longer... It is becoming a second-class service for people who can't afford to pay.'[20]

Communications

These concerns apply more generally to advice services, which have been struggling to maintain quality of service in the face of financial cutbacks and escalating levels of demand. The erosion of the advice network highlights another factor determining access to such services – the telecommunications network. Graham Murdock has underlined the importance of a telephone in providing easy access both to advice services and to social security offices, arguing that this is a key example of the relationship between communications and citizenship. The relatively low telephone ownership among poorer groups; charging policies that disadvantage call box users and those making local domestic calls; plus the reduction in the number of call boxes accepting cash – all have implications for the ability of poor people to exert their legal citizenship rights.[21]

The access problems specific to the large number of poor people living in rural areas are relevant here.[22] A contribution to a CPAG pamphlet on rural poverty observed that many rural areas 'lack facilities to enable people to exercise "the Fourth Right of Citizenship", that of reasonable access to information and advice'. For many villages 'advice and information can be obtained only at the cost of an expensive car journey, or an expensive telephone call to a service located outside the "local" call charge area'.[23]

The editor of the report, Alan Walker, concluded that the contributions to it 'point to a need to improve access to services and this in turn implies a better quality and coverage of public services in order to overcome inequalities between citizens based on geographical location'.[24]

Criminal justice

Although CPAG's legal work has primarily been concerned with the system of civil justice, questions of criminal justice also arise in the treatment of those alleged to be defrauding the social security system. Questions of civil liberties have been raised, in particular, by research into the operation of the cohabitation rule and the infamous Operation Major anti-fraud exercise.[25]

In *DHSS in Crisis,* Roger Smith deplored the trend towards random investigation of social security fraud on the basis that 'it is fundamentally at odds with the right of the citizen to be treated as innocent until proved guilty... There should be no sphere of life in which the citizen can be called in and subjected to interview to provide that he or she has not committed an offence.'[26]

Comparisons between the treatment of those accused of social security frauds and those accused of tax frauds indicate a differential assessment of their rights as citizens. The accumulating evidence of racism in the criminal justice system must also be a cause for concern from the perspective of the poor black citizen's 'right to justice'.[27]

Conclusion

The barriers to poor people asserting their legal rights on the one hand and the importance of clear entitlements to welfare on the other were central themes in the early work of CPAG. They inspired the establishment of the CRO as a demonstration project to encourage the development of similar rights agencies throughout the country. Since then, there has indeed been a significant expansion of welfare rights agencies of different kinds, and of a law centre network, although financial cutbacks have now put this expansion into reverse.

Yet large numbers of poor people still do not have access to the kind of advice and assistance they need to make a reality of their legal and welfare rights.

For poor people there can be a kind of negative feedback loop between their civil/legal and their social rights of citizenship. Inadequate and diminishing rights of social citizenship make it harder for poor people to exercise their rights of legal citizenship. Restrictions on the exercise of legal citizenship rights in the sphere of the welfare state undermine poor people's rights of social citizenship.

4

THE POLITICAL ELEMENT

By the political element I mean the right to participate in the exercise of political power, as a member of a body invested with political authority or as an elector of the members of such a body. [1]

T H Marshall

The distinction between the right and the ability to participate in political power as an expression of the citizen's socio-economic position has long been understood. Desmond King and Jeremy Waldron note that:

> Almost all the great theorists of citizenship ... have believed that in order to be a citizen of the polis, in order to be able to participate fully in public life, one needed to be in a certain socio-economic position... Two things have always been thought particularly important in this connection: the absence of great inequality and the possession of some modicum of wealth... Among theorists of citizenship, there has always been a consensus that some sort of rough equality among citizens is desirable. [2]

Of course, for the early theorists this did not extend to groups such as women and slaves who were clearly beyond the pale of citizenship.

While in the past the connection between citizenship and wealth or property has been used to justify the denial of political citizenship to certain groups, King and Waldron suggest that it can also be used to argue the opposite:

> If we are going to have universal citizenship in a political sense... then we should do it properly and see to it that everyone is put in the socio-economic position that we have reason to believe citizens ought to be in. In other words, if we take the ideal of universal suffrage seriously, then we should not be content simply to give everybody a vote; we should set about the task of giving them the economic security, which... is the necessary precondition for good citizenship. [3]

Economic exclusion from the political community

CPAG's *Excluding the Poor* explored the economic precondition for the effective exercise of political citizenship rights and marked the re-emergence of citizenship as an explicit theme in the work of CPAG. In a chapter on drawing the poverty line, the economist Meghnad Desai enunciates his first principle:

> Economic entitlement to an adequate living standard should be such that citizens can take full part in the political community. Not to give this is tantamount to a denial of political rights.[4]

Other contributions to the pamphlet show how inadequate living standards, combined with a consequent powerlessness, can indeed prevent poor citizens from taking full part in the political community. For example, Sue Ward describes how political activity creates demands and expectations which put subtle and often unnoticed pressures on those without the resources to meet them.

The distribution of time

Ward goes on to argue that apart from the financial costs associated with any form of activism, we must also consider the availability of time and opportunity. As she explains, the extent to which middle-class people are able to buy time with their money is often overlooked: 'Being poor takes up an enormous amount of time and energy.'[5] And these obstacles to political participation are doubled for women. The distribution of time between women and men is a crucial issue here.[6] The unpaid and time-consuming work of caring – be it for children or physically dependent adults – is carried out primarily by women and has serious implications for women's ability to exercise in full their political rights of citizenship.

In a study for CPAG, David Piachaud estimated that on average basic childcare tasks took about fifty hours a week. He found that even when 'the mother had no other job, the basic tasks occupied more hours than most men work in their jobs, and most mothers lacked *any* time free from childcare responsibilities'.[7]

A *Daily Telegraph* report of a Gallup Survey found that nearly three out of five women with families craved more time for themselves, and concluded that '"time poverty" is a growing problem for women'.[8] For lone mothers and other women in poverty – who cannot buy time for themselves, either by employing help or through the purchase of labour-saving goods – the problem of time is particularly acute.

The loss of political citizenship rights

Political citizenship is not just about active political participation; its bottom line is the exercise of the democratic right to vote. As a result of recent policy changes it is feared that a number of poor people will withdraw from the democratic process altogether. First, there have been a series of developments in social security, community care and housing policies which have resulted in growing numbers of poor people, particularly young people, living on the streets. Without an address, these people are not going to find their way on to the electoral register. Even those who have registered may well have moved several times by the time the next opportunity to vote arises.

Second are the implications of the poll tax (see Chapter 1). It is widely believed that a significant number of people will choose not to enrol on the electoral register in the hope that they will thereby evade registration for the poll tax:

> Because the poor are hit hardest by the poll tax and may, in many cases, be driven to desperation by the tax, it is they who are most likely to be tempted to give up their right to vote in the hope of evading the tax.[9]

There is evidence to suggest that this is already happening. In Scotland the number of people on the electoral register has dropped by about 26,000, only a third of which is attributable to population changes. Registration has fallen most markedly on the poorest housing estates. A survey of inner city local authorities in London found an unexpected drop in registration which is almost certainly due to fears about the poll tax.[10]

As well as losing the vote, withdrawal from the electoral register also means withdrawal from that other duty of citizenship – jury service. If there were to be a significant number of poor citizens not registering, this could have implications for the composition of juries.[11]

If the poll tax does result in a drop in the number of poor people who register to vote, it will serve to aggravate an existing problem. There is already evidence to suggest that levels of electoral registration are relatively low in inner city areas, particularly among the ethnic minority communities.[12]

The political marginalisation of the poor

It has been suggested that Britain could be going the way of the United States where 'low level participation by the poor and minorities sets up a vicious circle. Politicians try to attract, and frame policies to suit those who do or might vote for them. Thus an electorate heavily weighted towards the relatively affluent sets up pressures for economic policies which will benefit those groups.'[13]

After the 1987 election, a *Poverty* editorial warned of the dangers of a growing political as well as economic marginalisation of the poor. It quoted from an essay by Lord Blake, the Conservative historian:

> For long years past Conservatives in office or opposition have behaved nervously and cautiously on the assumption that they are the party of the 'haves', who are a minority, always under threat from the 'have-nots' who are a majority... Mrs Thatcher has instinctively realised that this dichotomy is no longer true. The 'haves' are in one sense now the majority.[14]

To the extent that the Opposition appears to have learnt the same lesson, the poor could face virtual disfranchisement.

The political marginalisation of the poor presents groups like CPAG with an enormous challenge. Indeed, the very existence of such organisations is a measure of the extent to which the political system has always muffled the voice of people in poverty: 'The history of the Child Poverty Action Group and other similar organisations in the late twentieth century is essentially one about the failings of British democracy.'[15]

Information as power

An important function of organisations like CPAG has been to compile and publicise information about poverty and inequality. It is a task which has become both more essential and more difficult as the Government seeks to obscure the facts and figures about social conditions in Britain from the public eye.

In his introduction to CPAG's social audit of the years 1979 to 1987, Alan Walker gave a number of 'examples of a consistent policy of obfuscation in order to cover up social reality and stifle public debate'.[16] Since then, growing concern amongst statisticians and the wider academic community about the manipulation of and access to official statistics has surfaced in the media. A former president of the Royal Statistical Society was quoted in the *Independent* as warning that 'informed public discussion of potentially controversial issues is being inhibited'.[17]

Accessible public information forms part of the 'infrastructure for citizenship' which facilitates informed democratic participation:[18]

> Communications and information are central to the exercise of full and effective citizenship in the contemporary era and should be regarded as part and parcel of citizenship rights.

The increasing application of market principles to the production and distribution of information is considered to be a threat to these rights. As the new technologies increasingly open up new forms of access for those with money, so are those without money further disadvantaged both as citizens and consumers:

> Whenever access to the communications and information resources required for full citizenship depend upon purchasing power (as expressed directly through customer payments or indirectly through the unequal distribution of advertising subsidies to production) substantial inequalities are generated, which undermine the nominal universality of citizenship.

As a result of growing income inequality the poor 'suffer from a double disadvantage. They are priced out of the market for new services, and left with an infrastructure of public provision which is either unable or unwilling to provide the full range of resources for citizenship.'[19]

As Golding and Murdock point out, the issue of differential access to information takes on an added urgency in the face of restrictions on the flow of official information.

A junior minister recently told the House of Commons that one of the 'requirements of personal and social education under the national curriculum is education in citizenship. Surely both sides of the House should welcome the obligation placed on schools to educate children to participate in our democratic process.'[20]

If the Government genuinely wants all sections of the community to exercise the democratic rights and duties of citizenship, it must remove the material obstacles that are simultaneously being erected as a result of a range of its policy initiatives.

Conclusion

The exercise of political citizenship rights is determined, in part, by economic and social factors. Lack of resources and a consequent powerlessness can prevent poor citizens from playing a full and active role in the public political community. In the case of women, this is aggravated by the distribution of time and tasks in the 'private' sphere of the home. The most fundamental political citizenship right – that of the vote – is threatened for some groups in poverty by the poll tax and growing homelessness. There is a danger that this could worsen the political marginalisation suffered by the poor. At the same time, the 'infrastructure for citizenship' (accessible public information) is being eroded and is increasingly subject to the principles of the market. Such policies are inconsistent with the Government's declared desire to encourage education for citizenship.

5

THE SOCIAL ELEMENT

By the social element I mean the whole range from the right to a modicum of economic welfare and security to the right to share to the full in the social heritage and to live the life of a civilised being, according to the standard prevailing in the society.[1]
                                                               T H Marshall

A key facet of the social element of citizenship for Marshall and subsequent writers has been that it offers a 'universal right to real income which is not proportionate to the market value of the claimant'.[2] It creates 'the common floor on which everybody stands'.[3] As such, social citizenship rights have the potential to challenge the inequalities generated by the wages system (although, as we shall see, in practice they can mirror as well as modify those inequalities).

Contemporary writers on citizenship have noted that 'the welfare state is the most institutional embodiment of social citizenship rights'.[4] They argue that citizenship theory 'offers a distinct moral justification of the welfare state ... [which] is rooted in a conception of what it is to be a full member of a community and the social rights that are necessary to protect and reinforce that membership'.[5]

Harris has also pointed to a confusion in this moral justification between rights and altruism. Pursuing a similar theme, Michael Ignatieff argues passionately that 'the language of citizenship is not properly about compassion at all, since compassion is a private virtue which cannot be legislated or enforced. The practice of citizenship is about ensuring everyone the entitlement necessary to the exercise of their liberty. As a political question, welfare is about rights, not caring.'[6]

Contributors to *Critical Social Policy* have argued that the next step is to tie these citizenship rights and entitlements to the fulfilment of need. This implies 'not just a set of rights but the power to achieve needs, in terms of access to resources'.[7] It is also suggested that 'despite existing differences, we do all have certain basic needs which can be the basis of demands for welfare rights; and which challenge openly those who wish to maintain current forms of exclusion to justify these in political debate'.[8]

Elsewhere it has been argued that through this dual emphasis on rights and needs 'citizenship can have a unifying function'. In this context, needs are defined as 'the universal preconditions for creative and fulfilling human action. All people, whatever their gender, age, nation, class, religion, ethnicity, have basic needs which, if unsatisfied, will prevent them acting successfully within the societies where they live.' Health and autonomy ('the consciousness and skills to participate fully in social life with self-respect and the respect of one's peers') are identified as the two fundamental human needs, the achievement of which requires the satisfaction of certain intermediate needs such as an adequate diet and housing.[9] However, any more precise identification of these 'intermediate needs' might reveal considerable differences of perception between women and men.[10]

The conceptualisation of social citizenship rights as a set of entitlements underpinning certain broad universal needs raises questions about the limitations of existing citizenship rights, both for those excluded by poverty and for other marginalised groups:

> A contemporary 'politics of citizenship' must take into account the role which the social movements have played in expanding the claims to rights and entitlements to new areas. It must address not only the issues of class and inequality, but also questions of membership posed by feminism, the black and ethnic minority movements, ecology ... and vulnerable minorities like children.[11]

The potential tension between the recognition of diversity and difference and the universal, integrative functions of citizenship has to be addressed. Similarly, a recognition of diversity raises questions about the common 'social heritage' embodied in Marshall's definition of the social element of citizenship. The key may lie partly in Marshall's own emphasis on equality of status, reinterpreted as mutual respect.[12]

At the material level, the challenge is to integrate diversity and difference into universal rights of social citizenship:

For citizenship theory, the goal is not homogeneity; the enemy is not heterogeneity. The goal is to provide everyone with the wherewithal to enjoy and participate in the benefits of pluralism. The enemy is only those differences which are connected to the processes of exclusion and domination.

Harris suggests that this exclusion can be identified regardless of cultural differences because there are 'common elements underlying cultural variations which can effectively define minimum standards below which individuals and families are cut off from the rest of society'.[13] This is a similar thesis to that advanced by the Sheffield Group.

We turn now to a consideration of some of these processes of exclusion which have been central to CPAG's work. The initial focus of this work was primarily the exclusion of poor children and their families within a universalistic framework which attempted to integrate their needs with those of families generally. Since then, the Group's understanding of exclusion from full citizenship has gradually broadened and deepened to incorporate the dimensions of gender and race.

Excluding the poor

In *Citizenship*, Barbalet defined the concept in terms of participation in and exclusion from the life of the community:

> Citizenship can readily be described as participation in, or membership of, a community ... the struggle for citizenship has been the struggle against the inequalities which exclusion produces.[14]

Understood in these terms, the struggle for citizenship is by no means over. CPAG's *Excluding the Poor* made clear that when one catalogues 'the demands made by political, economic and social institutions on those who would engage fully in the society around them, it becomes clear that poverty is most comprehensively understood as a condition of partial citizenship'.[15]

Poor people lack the resources to 'fulfil what is expected of them at the workplace, in the home, the family and the community and as local as well as national citizens'.[16]

Excluding the Poor also underlined how poverty curtails another important element of social citizenship: rights as 'opportunities to make choices'.[17] This has important implications for the extent to which poor people can enjoy genuine freedoms.

In a recent *Poverty* editorial, Fran Bennett uses Dahrendorf's analogy of citizenship as a set of 'entry tickets' to participation in society, and goes on to argue 'that a significant number of Britain's population are excluded from "full citizenship" and a fair share of the country's growing wealth'.[18]

A similar point is the central theme of a pamphlet published recently by the Methodist Church:

> ...the least well-off in our society are being detached from the mainland of general prosperity in such a way as to mock the idea of belonging to one another, or a shared citizenship.[19]

Earlier, the authors of the *Faith in the City* report wrote of having seen degrees of poverty and inequality exceeding 'the limits that would be thought acceptable by most of our fellow citizens'.[20]

From time to time, CPAG has conducted studies of the living standards of families living in poverty and these have provided graphic and painful evidence of how lives are diminished by the poverty that excludes.[21] The most recent, published by Tyneside CPAG, concludes that:

> The picture which emerges from this detailed study of family lives is one of constant restriction in almost every aspect of people's activities... The lives of these families, and perhaps most seriously, the lives of the children in them, are marked by the unrelieved struggle to manage, with dreary diets and drab clothing. They also suffer what amounts to cultural imprisonment in their home in our society in which getting out with money to spend on recreation and leisure is normal at every other income level... Clearly the level of benefit is not enough to allow ordinary families to share in conventional living standards.[22]

Other reports have documented the manner in which social citizenship rights have been particularly undermined in certain parts of the UK – most notably, Northern Ireland[23] – and for specific groups of claimants – notably the unemployed. CPAG has criticised both economic policies which have eroded the key post-war citizenship right to employment (for men at least) and social policies which have treated the unemployed 'as if they were an inferior caste'.[24] Similarly, the Disability Alliance, of which CPAG is a member, has repeatedly drawn attention to how the failure of social policies has meant the continued exclusion from full participation for many people with disabilities.[25]

The concepts of exclusion and participation, which are integral to that of social citizenship, help us to understand the meaning of continued poverty in the midst of an ever-more-affluent society. In one of the very earliest editions of *Poverty*, CPAG warned that rising national income would not automatically abolish poverty; on the contrary, 'it may well add to the burdens of the poor as more and more things that were once luxuries have become conventional necessities'.[26]

As the costs of full citizenship participation increase, so has the gap between the ability of the poor and that of the rest of the community to meet these costs widened. Moreover, if we take the benefit rates provided by the means-tested safety net for those not in full-time work as a measure of the basic level of participation guaranteed (albeit very imperfectly) by society, then we find that the number of people excluded from this level of participation is higher now than in the 1960s when CPAG was founded. According to Peter Townsend and David Gordon, the proportion of the population living below the supplementary benefit/national assistance level in 1985 (4.5 per cent) was double that in 1960 (2.3 per cent).[27]

The corollary of exclusion from full participation is often exclusion from public consciousness. It has been argued that one element of the relationship between communications and citizenship is the ability for all citizens to recognise themselves in the range of representations on offer.[28] An important role of the poverty lobby has always been to ensure that the reality of modern day poverty is adequately and fairly represented in the media. This has never been easy. A recent problem has been the attempt by some politicians to exclude the poor altogether from the public representations of our society. Michael Harrington has warned that one of the major challenges facing anti-poverty campaigners in the US is the attempt to define poverty out of existence.[29] In the UK, the latest twist is the

Prime Minister's concern not to 'denigrate' those on income support by labelling them as poor.

At local level too, some local authorities (not just Conservative) have been anxious not to tarnish their new image of enterprise with anything so depressing as poverty.[30] The most extreme example of this phenomenon is perhaps to be found in Bradford where the closure of the Benefit Shops was partly justified on the grounds that they occupied prime sites 'which should be used to convey a more positive image of the city', in contrast to the image of 'dependency' which they allegedly conveyed.[31] What is at issue here is not the presentation of a positive image of a particular city but the attempt to erase the reality experienced by a significant number of its citizens. In this way the exclusion from full citizenship associated with poverty is intensified and the needs of poor citizens are subordinated to the maintenance of that positive image.[32]

Black second class citizens

The absence of fair representation in the media and the community in general is a particularly acute issue for black citizens for whom the whole concept of citizenship can be a double-edged sword. Richard Holme has referred to the 'narrow and repressive sense in which the word is used in questions of race and immigration by the Home Office'.[33] At a time when citizenship rights have been eroded to the particular detriment of black people, it is this 'narrow and repressive sense' which will tend to come to mind even if, as British citizens, they are not directly affected. At the same time, regardless of legal citizenship, black people may still be 'denied many of the advantages of membership of the community through the attitudes and actions of the white majority'.[34]

The treatment of poor black people in this country has to be understood in the context of a succession of immigration and nationality laws which have amounted to 'the systematic withdrawal of rights from black Commonwealth citizens'.[35] Within the last decade, the 1981 Nationality Act removed the right to British citizenship by virtue of birth on British soil and deprived Commonwealth citizens settled here since 1973 of their automatic right to register as British citizens. The citizenship registration and naturalisation fees were also significantly increased, an issue taken up by CPAG and other groups. In *Passport to Benefits* examples are given of people who have been prevented from acquiring British citizenship because they could not afford the fee.[36] Most recently, the 1988 Immigration Act abolished the right of British and long-settled Commonwealth citizen men to be joined by their wives and children. Entry will now be permitted only where such citizens can prove that they can maintain their families without 'recourse to public funds' (defined as the main weekly means-tested benefits and accommodation under the Housing Act 1985 Part III [Housing the Homeless]). By removing the only right to family unity in British immigration law, the 1988 Act has aggravated the problem of divided families, and cast doubts on the sincerity of the Government's vocal concern for the well-being of the 'family'.

This extension of the 'recourse to public funds' rule represents a further link in the chain that ties elements of welfare law to immigration law. The chain itself was forged as an integral part of the development of welfare policy, as Fiona Williams has documented:

> Paranoia that immigrants might scrounge from 'our welfare' was written into many of the policies of the welfare reforms of the 1920s, 1930s and 1940s.[37]

The corollary of increasingly restrictive immigration controls over the past decade has been an added emphasis on internal controls through 'the welfare state, in which entitlement to education, social security and other benefits and services has become increasingly dependent upon immigration status and in which it has become legitimate for a range of officials to question claimants and others about their status and thus to act as agents of immigration control'.[38]

Such insidious policies have meant a growth in the indiscriminate passport-checking of black claimants, all of whom are at risk of being assumed to be a recent immigrant, even if born or long-settled in this country. The subjection of new income support claimants who have been in the country for less than five years to detailed questioning about their immigration status formalises the process of passport-checking.*[39]

---

*The use of documentation checking by the DSS as a form of control has also been criticised with regard to the treatment of 'travellers' as 'less than average citizens'.[40]

A CPAG pamphlet on the general question of race and social security suggested that one result of passport checks 'is that some black people see the DSS as, in effect, an arm of the immigration department of the Home Office, and do not, therefore, claim benefit for fear that their own immigration status may be questioned. This is so, even though they may have nothing to fear.'

There has been particular criticism of the provision introduced under the 1980 Social Security Act, whereby financial responsibility for an immigrant admitted under the sponsorship system lies with the sponsor. Black claimants 'are not just treated as second-class citizens – as are most claimants – but they are second class even among claimants. In this respect, the sponsorship provisions are particularly iniquitous. This is not just because they are open to misunderstanding and misapplication, but, more important, because they create a class of people who may be in the UK quite lawfully – indeed, who may be fully settled here, but who are entitled to welfare on the same basis as other citizens only if they are prepared to risk legal action against relatives who have sponsored them.'[41]

The second-class treatment of black citizens by the social security system is then compounded by its failure 'to take account of and make provision for the different customs, cultures and languages of many black people who are forced to claim benefits',[42] and by the racist attitudes displayed by some DSS officers.[43] It is clear that 'this cannot inspire black people with the confidence that they will be treated correctly and given their rightful entitlement'.[44]

The facts of racial disadvantage are evidenced by a disproportionately high incidence of unemployment and low pay among the minority communities. In a recent *Poverty* article, Kenneth Leech and Kaushika Amin argue that 'it is clear that there has been an increased "racialisation" of poverty ... [that] blackness and poverty are more correlated than they were some years ago'.[45]

This 'racialisation' of poverty has clear implications for the black community, inhibiting them from effectively exercising their rights of citizenship. The Chair of the CRE has also warned of the danger of fostering a sense of powerlessness and hopelessness among black people excluded from a decent education, employment and housing.[46] It is increasingly clear that racial harassment and violence are contributing to this exclusion. A Home Office report has warned that 'if the fear of racial harassment deprives people from ethnic minorities of the freedom of choice over such fundamental matters as where they live or work, or if they are reluctant to leave home to take their children to school, to visit a doctor, to use public transport or libraries or parks, then they will be unable to play their full part in the life of this country or to feel that they have a stake in its future.' [47]

It has been argued that 'racial attacks, racial harassment, and the threat of them are thus very significant in perpetuating second class welfare citizenship for black people in Britain.' [48] In addition, as we have already noted, the disproportionate impact of the poll tax on minority communities constitutes a further threat to their citizenship rights (see Chapter 4).

The preamble to the European Community Charter of Fundamental Social Rights declares that 'it is important to combat every form of social exclusion and discrimination, including discrimination on the grounds of race, colour and religion.' However, the Charter contains no specific articles which would make this aim a reality, and many of its provisions are restricted to European Community citizens, thereby excluding many who are resident non-citizens.[49] Moreover, a number of commentators fear that racist policies are 'likely to be compounded as Britain moves towards greater integration with the rest of the European Community and as the Community as a whole adopts an increasingly xenophobic and racist stance towards Third World countries and their peoples'.[50]

There is also cause for concern over the likely consequences of the removal of border immigration controls between EEC countries:

> ...an immigration status which would formerly have been checked at a frontier checkpoint will become an immigration status which might be checked anywhere and on any occasion... In claiming social security benefits, registering for health care, starting new employment, or even just walking or driving down the street, the demand 'to see your passport' is likely to become ubiquitous under a harmonised regime of restrictive immigration controls.[51]

The threat to the rights of black citizens of Europe is all too plain.

The concept of social citizenship has the potential for uniting black and white people in poverty, in their demand for adequate social and economic rights. But first, its negative connotations, associated with current immigration and nationality laws, will have to be removed by the development of non-racist laws governing entry and citizenship at both UK and European levels.

Female second class citizens

A full understanding of the relationship between poverty and the social element of citizenship must take into account women's greater vulnerability to poverty:

> ...the conditions under which women obtain access to resources, the levels of those resources, women's control over resources, and their degree of responsibility for the welfare of others in deploying material resources - all these are factors which make women more vulnerable to poverty and which shape women's experience of the impact of poverty.[52]

For many women, poverty is closely related, either directly or indirectly, to financial dependence on men. This dependence is both a cause and a product of their poverty and, at the same time, legitimises women's inferior economic position.[53] In this way the ideology of dependency affects even those women not directly dependent on men – for example, lone mothers and many Afro-Caribbean women.

The implications of women's dependency for their rights as citizens are profound. Yet Marshall completely ignored the issue, as have many subsequent citizenship theorists.[54] There is not the space here to develop this point in depth. The focus therefore will be narrowed down to women's position in the social security system.

In 1943, Elizabeth Abbott and Katherine Bompas attacked the Beveridge Plan for treating the married woman as a dependant of her husband: 'no independent status is given to her as citizen and worker'.[55] Three decades later, Barbara Castle referred to married women as 'second class citizens entitled to third class benefits'.[56] Since then, direct discrimination has been removed from the social security system, largely thanks to the EEC directive on Equal Treatment for Men and Women. However, 'in practice, equal treatment does little to guarantee equal outcome'.[57] In at least one case (the severe disablement allowance) this is because it is arguable that direct discrimination has simply been replaced by indirect discrimination.[58] More fundamental, though, is the fact that integral features of both the contributory and means-tested benefit systems disadvantage women.

Entitlement to contributory benefits depends on previous employment status. Hilary Land has argued that such a system which treats 'women as individuals like men can only be partially successful in meeting women's needs since women do not behave like men in the labour market: their employment patterns are different' because of the unequal division of caring responsibilities within the family.[59] Thus many women's contribution records suffer as a result of their interrupted employment patterns. Many other women are excluded from the scheme altogether because of earnings below the contribution threshold, even though the married women's option not to contribute started to be phased out over a decade ago.[60] Unless they are widows, lone mothers are not even covered by the scheme. Despite this, the insurance principle is frequently held up as the epitome of citizenship:

> The basis of citizenship of entitlement was the insurance principle and universality of benefit: *everyone* contributed and *everyone* benefited. [emphasis added][61]

Despite the inadequacies of the contributory system, it has at least enabled some women to build up an entitlement to benefit in their own right. However, that entitlement has been eroded by recent changes which have tightened up some of the contribution conditions and cut back on some of the contributory benefits. It has been suggested that this is an example of a Europe-wide response to the Equal Treatment Directive, in which policies have been shifted towards 'family based, means-tested social assistance, which indirectly discriminates against women through the apparently gender-neutral concepts of "breadwinner" or "head of household"'.[62]

Whether or not this shift is simply a direct response to the Directive (and in this country, at least, it reflects a more fundamental ideological shift) the effect is certainly to disadvantage women. Even though married women are now entitled to claim means-tested benefits on behalf of themselves and their families, that entitlement is dependent on a household means-test that takes no account of the distribution of resources within the family.[63] Moreover, in the case of income support, it is still generally the man who claims benefit.

The most recent draft EEC Directive on equal treatment proposes individual entitlement to benefits as one possible step forward. It is only through individual rights to benefit that married and cohabiting women will be able to enjoy genuine citizenship rights under the social security scheme. Rights mediated by their partners cease to be genuine rights. Some might argue that this will simply increase women's dependency on the state. However, Robert E Goodin has argued that 'the sort of dependencies that occur within families are morally more objectionable than the dependencies that occur between citizen and State, at least insofar as the citizen's entitlements come in the form of rights.'[64]

A move towards individual benefits, if it is genuinely to benefit women, will have to mean a move away from means-tests and contribution tests towards contingency-based benefits. This then raises the question of which contingencies are to be covered and in particular the difficult question of how the work of caring within the family is to be recognised without reinforcing the sexual division of labour and trapping women in the home. The answer cannot lie solely in the social security system. It must also embrace a coherent policy for the expansion of good quality childcare facilities for school-age as well as pre-school children and a set of employment rights, such as those contained in the EEC Draft Directive on Parental Leave and Leave for Family Reasons, vetoed by the UK Government. Overall, such a package should make it easier for both women and men to combine paid employment with caring responsibilities and thereby enhance women's position as full citizens and reduce their vulnerability to poverty. The example of our European partners and the European Social Charter's call for 'the development of amenities enabling those concerned to reconcile their occupational and family obligations more easily' might facilitate progress in this direction.

The rights of the child

A central theme of a CPAG/NCCL pamphlet on family policy was that 'there is no inherent conflict between a better deal for families, the rights of women and the rights of children'.[65] One example of where the rights of children and of their mothers coincide is child benefit. The origins of child benefit lie in the case for the endowment of motherhood made by women such as Eleanor Rathbone. This case was made explicitly with reference to the citizenship claims of both mother and child. Thus, for example, Beveridge wrote that family allowances 'meant that part of the total national income ... should be assigned to those individual citizens who are undertaking the rearing of the citizens of the future'.[66]

Some of the arguments for a universal benefit for children put forward earlier this century were echoed recently by Marina Warner:

> ...the point about universal benefits is that they affirm the value of such social tasks as having children, rearing them, or caring for relatives; they make benefits themselves an expression of collective approval for the endeavour, not begrudged hand-outs, stigmatising the recipients as beggars and failures... The introduction of selective principles brutally underlines differences between families, when childhood should be a time of equality, of possibility, if not background circumstances.[67]

Lurking behind much of the current debate about the future of child benefit are very different perceptions of children's value and their role in society. First, notes Hermione Parker, 'those whose aim is poverty relief tend to be those who regard children as an "expensive hobby" which "parents have chosen to have".' Joan Brown argues that this attitude devalues 'children who are human beings with their own human rights'.[68] A recent manifestation has been the 'baby-hype' of the late 1980s in which children have become 'the latest must-have accessory' but definitely for private consumption only, with complaints in the press about 'the obstacles that conspire to turn British parents with children into second class citizens' in restaurants and the like.[69] The CPAG/NCCL pamphlet goes on to argue that, 'despite the lip-service paid to children, they are not, in our society, treated as valued or valuable human beings, but as second class or even third class citizens.'[70] In contrast, 'those whose aim is poverty prevention take a wider view. They think of children as junior citizens, who did not choose to be born, and upon whom all our futures depend.'[71]

This view was expressed graphically by a mother who wrote to the Save Child Benefit campaign: 'Children are the seed corn of any society ... it is not in the nation's interests to neglect the needs of its future citizens.'[72]

Child benefit represents a badge of citizenship. Its erosion and its uncertain future are one indicator of the extent to which this nation continues to neglect the needs of its future citizens. Another is the large number of children whose childhood years are being blighted by poverty.

The second edition of *Poverty* published posed a set of urgent questions regarding children living below the social assistance level:

> At least half a million children in Britain have experienced poverty and deprivation for ninety days since our first issue. Things are moving – but how fast? Must they face another ninety days of poverty? A year? Two years? Must we tell half a million children to be patient, to accept the drab, cheerless existence, which is all they have ever known, until the rest of us – the prosperous ones – are ready to open the gates of opportunity?[73]

Two decades later, the number of children living below social assistance level had not significantly diminished and the number of children being raised on social assistance has increased from about half a million, when CPAG was founded, to over two million today. The gates of opportunity have remained firmly closed. The basic rights of social citizenship including adequate health care, shelter and food are not guaranteed to these children. As a result, many do not even survive their first year, since relatively high rates of infant and perinatal mortality persist at the bottom of the social scale.

This denial of full rights of citizenship is perhaps at its most acute – and most conspicuous – amongst the growing number of young people who are living as beggars on the streets. A recent NACAB report on the effects of the new benefits regime on 16/17-year-olds concluded:

> The combination of major restrictions on rights to and levels of benefit, coupled frequently with seriously inadequate advice about what rights they have, produced a situation which is intolerable in a society committed to the welfare of all its citizens.[74]

Many of these young people will have been in care. For some the wheel will have come full circle, for it is poverty that separates many children from their parents in the first place. This further example of the corrosive effect of poverty on the citizenship rights of children was documented in *Inequalities in Childcare* and confirmed by the

Social Services Select Committee which accepted that 'there is a well established link between deprivation and children coming into care'.[75]

The exclusion of poorer children from full citizenship is becoming more pronounced, not just because of the overall growing divide between them and the rest of society, but also because childhood has become an increasingly costly business: 'the market's dream is to make every child expensive; children have become a consumer target, through their parents' pockets and their guilt.'[76] The resultant pressures on poor families are enormous in a society where consumer goods have become 'symbols of citizenship'.[77]

These costs can also pertain to another important gateway to citizenship – the education system. A recurrent theme of CPAG's work over the years has been the costliness of our 'free' education system to the detriment of the full participation of poor children. A recent development in this particular form of exclusion is the expectation under the National Curriculum that children aged five plus should know about computers. With even toy computers costing between £25 and £70, poor children without access to home computers are bound to be at a disadvantage.[78] At the same time, it has been reported that the parental contribution to the implementation of the National Curriculum stands at about £90 million compared with the £10 million spent this financial year by the Department of Education and Science on the core curriculum.[79] This growing reliance on parental contributions will widen the gap between the facilities for children in poorer and better-off areas, again eroding the floor of common citizenship that the State education system should be providing. The inequalities in our education system are then compounded when, in the absence of a statutory educational maintenance allowance scheme, children from poorer families tend to leave school at the earliest opportunity.[80]

The denial to so many of our children of the full fruits of the affluent society in which they live has raised questions about how the UK's record will stand up against the principles contained in the UN Declaration of the Rights of the Child due to come into force this year.[81] Dominic Byrne of Save the Children Fund has described the origins of the Declaration as 'the belief that all children have rights and expectations as citizens, irrespective of race, creed and nationality'.[82] He also emphasises the potential value for children in this country of the Declaration's Articles covering the rights of children to benefit from social security and an adequate standard of living. In a *Guardian* article, Byrne concluded that 'full international recognition of children's rights has been a long time coming. But making these rights a reality will depend on how vigorously and creatively children's agencies are, in both the State and voluntary sectors, in the use of the opportunities presented by the Convention.'[83]

The rights of children are qualitatively different from those of adults. Although they are members of the community, children are not full citizens in the sense of the political and legal rights which pertain to citizenship; the social rights of citizenship come to them indirectly through the adults responsible for their care. That, in itself, imposes an obligation on society both to protect them and to provide the resources necessary for their care and development. In this way, the citizenship rights of children discussed here merge with their human rights of which the adult society acts as guardian.

The social rights of citizenship

The introduction of the family allowance as a citizenship benefit reflected a wider commitment to the ideal of citizenship in the establishment of the post-war welfare state. In July 1948, Attlee told the nation that the new social security benefits being introduced were 'comprehensive and available to every citizen' and the 1950 Labour Party Manifesto declared that 'Labour has honoured the pledge made in 1945 to make social security the birthright of every citizen'.[84]

As noted already, such claims ignored completely the birthright of many female citizens and the more general limitations of an insurance-based scheme (see below). However, they were important in creating a vision of a social security system which should not rely on the hated means test. The Beveridge Report thus frequently evoked the notion of common citizenship as part of its case against continued reliance on means-tested assistance.

For Marshall, universal benefits and services were an important means of achieving the 'equality of status' which he identified with the social element of citizenship. In the first pamphlet published by CPAG, Richard Titmuss made the case for:

comprehensive universal services available as of right to everyone by virtue of citizenship. They are a fundamental prerequisite for the growth of a compassionate and civilised society based on self-respect and respect for the rights of others. I do not believe we can advance towards these objectives by institutionalising wholly selective means-tested services for poor people – for a separated group of citizens – whether we are talking about social security, education, medical care or other services. All historical experience in Britain and other countries over the past fifty years has demonstrated, again and again, that separate, selective services for poor people (the less eligible citizens) are poor services.[85]

Titmuss feared that he would be branded 'a social policy square' in talking about the 'rights and responsibilities of citizenship'. Yet many would agree that his message is still relevant today. The case he made for universality still has a resonance, since it can be argued that 'universal benefits contribute to a nation's sense of community and interdependence - to national solidarity',[86] whereas means-testing 'may be perceived (both by recipients and the public) as involving second-class citizenship'.[87]

However, the citizenship ideal was not sufficient to achieve the Beveridge goal of 'security against want without a means test'. One important reason was the failure of successive governments to provide adequate non-means-tested benefits. Another was that the embodiment of that ideal – the national insurance scheme – created a limited and exclusive citizenship right:

The citizenship principle is limited insofar as rights are dependent on contributions which are linked to the ability to earn ... and reflect the standard of living a man [sic] can win for himself within the market situation, rather than his status as a citizen.[88]

Hermione Parker has argued vigorously that citizenship rather than a contribution record should be the main basis for establishing entitlement to social security. She points to growing support for this view even amongst those who favour reform within the present system, rather than a new basic income scheme which would be the ultimate citizenship benefit:

...the *sine qua non* for poverty prevention is the replacement of social insurance and its attendant contribution conditions by a simple test of citizenship of legal residence, as is already the case with child benefit. Social insurance is a system of exclusion, because those who are not insured, or who have not paid sufficient contributions, or who fail any of the other manifold requirements, are ineligible or receive substandard amounts. Despite its clear achievements, social insurance is not, never has been and never can be a sufficient guarantee against poverty.[89]

As she notes, social insurance serves to mirror the inequalities of the labour market to the advantage of the strong and the detriment of the weak.[90]

The ideal of citizenship also lay behind the emphasis placed by groups like CPAG on benefit being paid as a right. A *Poverty* editorial in 1967 stated:

Respect for human dignity requires respect for human rights. Paupers are no longer deprived of the rights of citizenship. In more subtle ways, however, the poor are still made to feel that society regards them as a burden – as having needs rather than rights... In this way, money is used not to confer status but to take it away. That is why the Child Poverty Action Group has increasingly stressed the need not only for adequate incomes but for greater emphasis on the legal rights of low-income families.[91]

Similarly, Titmuss wrote in his contribution to a CPAG pamphlet on rights that 'this question of the right to social security by virtue of citizenship is part of the wider and more fundamental problem of defining the "Good Society"... The social policy of the Good Society will attempt, in principle and in practice, as far as is possible, to trust rather than distrust people; to accord to them "rights" rather than "charity".'[92]

What is at stake here is how our fellow citizens are treated. A recurrent theme in the work of CPAG has been the second-class service provided to many social security claimants, particularly through the social assistance scheme. Others have pointed to a 'crisis of service delivery' in the welfare state, a large part of which lies 'in the relationship between the citizens and the state and the institutions of the state'.[93] Ignatieff traces this relationship back to the emphasis in the post-war citizenship ideal on a 'passive quality of entitlement at the expense of the active equality of participation. The entitled were never empowered because empowerment would have infringed the prerogatives of the managers of the welfare state.'

One result has been that the Right has been able to harness the consequent disenchantment with welfare services in its recasting of the welfare relationship to fit a model of consumerism rather than of citizenship. It is argued that the failure of welfare bureaucracies will 'continue to dog any future politics of citizenship that fails to think clearly about the dilemmas of accountability and representation'.[94]

While there are clear limits to the degree of 'user control' possible in a centralised system like social security, there are ways in which the delivery of the service at a local level, at least, can be made more accountable to users.

The new emphasis on the need to empower users of welfare services is important. Nevertheless, it should not be forgotten that, to the extent that the powerlessness of the poor is a function of lack of money, one means of empowerment is to provide poor people with more money. This can be achieved partly by strengthening economic rights of citizenship through, for example, minimum wages legislation and improved access to decent jobs for vulnerable groups in the labour market. But it must also be recognised that there will always be some people who have no choice but to rely on social security for their main source of income. For them, the benefit provided by the social security system must be sufficiently high to guarantee their citizenship rights and facilitate the fulfilment of their citizenship obligations.

In *Social Welfare and the Art of Giving*, Titmuss posed the question:

> What matters then, what indeed is fundamental to the health of welfare, the objective towards which its face is set? To universalise humanistic ethics and the social rights of citizenship, or to divide, discriminate and compete?[95]

Although the vision of post-war citizenship set its face towards the former, its partial and limited conception of citizenship meant that it could not live up to its own ideals.

Now the welfare state is facing in the opposite direction and becoming 'an instrument of division rather than solidarity; and better paid, regularly organised workers are being drawn into the market sector, with their interests as ratepayers and taxpayers opposed to the excluded, casualised sector of welfare beneficiaries'.[96]

These beneficiaries are being increasingly stigmatised as 'dependent on the benefits culture'; the citizenship ideal of universalism is receding ever further as means-testing is now promoted as a positive virtue in its place; the social fund marks a retreat from a commitment to welfare rights and, instead, increased reliance on charity in an attempt to reduce poor citizens' expectations of their legitimate claims on the State; and the growing emphasis on private provision, subsidised by public tax relief, could signal the final 'collapse of the post-war tradition of welfare citizenship' if use of State provision comes to 'signify membership of a social minority rather than citizenship'.[97]

It is perhaps a testimony to the strength and resilience of the citizenship ideal that, despite its imperfect incarnation in the post-war welfare state and its gradual demise as a principle guiding social policy, it is now acting as inspiration once more to those who want to rebuild the welfare state on the foundations of justice and democratic participation.

Conclusion

A key element in the post-war vision of citizenship was participation in the life of the community of which one is a member. Poverty, which, in contrast, spells exclusion from full participation, diminishes the citizenship rights of a significant proportion of the community. These rights are all too often eroded further for black people, women and people with disabilities. Although children are not full citizens, the community acts as a guardian of their rights. The UN Declaration of the Rights of the Child holds up a mirror to our society, revealing the extent to which many children are being denied the fruits of the affluent society in which they are growing up.

The persistence of wide-scale poverty in our society is a measure of the failure of the post-war social security system to make a reality of the ideals of social citizenship which it embodied. Littered with means tests and contribution tests, it accommodated and sometimes mirrored the inequalities of the wages system, rather than seriously challenging them. It is now moving further and further away from the citizenship principles which inspired it. Looking forward, the need is being reasserted for a form of social citizenship which will embody the principles of social justice and accountability and reconcile the demands of universalism with those of the different groups that make up our community.

CONCLUSION

THE FUTURE OF CITIZENSHIP

'Public morality is back on the agenda' declared the *Sunday Times* in its editorial to mark the publication of Charles Murray's essay on 'the British underclass'.[1]

However, the solution to the problem of 'the underclass' proposed by Murray and the *Sunday Times* – the regulation of individual behaviour by means of the restoration of social stigma – lies ultimately in the sphere of private rather than public morality. In this, it reflects current attempts on the Right to fashion a notion of citizenship which appeals to individual responsibility – be it the responsibility of poor citizens to stand on their own two feet or of the better-off 'active' citizens, who have benefited from the economic growth and income tax cuts of recent years to do good.

Few would deny that citizenship involves obligations as well as rights. But the two must be in balance. What is happening today is that obligations are being emphasised at the expense of rights. Behind the eulogy to the private citizen and her or his responsibilities, the public citizen and the public rights of citizenship are being buried.

It has been a central argument of this book that it is not possible to divorce the rights and responsibilities which are supposed to unite citizens from the inequalities of power and resources that divide them. These inequalities – particularly of class, race and gender – run like fault-lines through our society and shape the contours of citizenship in the civil, political and social spheres. Poverty spells exclusion from the full rights of citizenship in each of these spheres and undermines people's ability to fulfil the private and public obligations of citizenship. For people with disabilities, this exclusion is often compounded. The exclusion of millions of our fellow citizens from the enjoyment of the full fruits of citizenship that a wealthy society like ours can provide is an issue for public, not private, morality. Exhortations to private charity and to self-reliance at best serve merely to paper over the deepening fault-lines; at worst they accentuate the inequalities of power and status that feed them, while other policies are eroding social citizenship rights.

In contrast, the resurrection of the citizenship ideal, expressed in the language of social justice (and located firmly in the sphere of public morality), could potentially provide the basis for building a more united society. If this is to happen, it first must be transformed from the monolithic concept of the post-war citizenship theorists to one which embodies, in particular, the dimensions of race and gender.

The public citizenship ideal stems from an idea of 'the common good':

> ...citizenship embodies a concept of the common good which appeals not to highly specific and sectional goals, but to a set of needs, rights, resources and opportunities which all individuals must have to pursue any goals at all in our sort of society.[2]

Through the notion of 'a social morality which is self-interested'[3] it attempts to bridge the apparently unbridgeable gulf between individual self-interest and the common good. This thesis has been developed by Bill Jordan who has argued that 'there is a tradition which has identified membership of society – citizenship – as the basis of the common good, and hence as indispensable to any form of social morality or good society. According to this tradition, the State must ensure that certain assets are distributed in such a way that all citizens have an interest in contributing to, as well as benefiting from, particular social goods.'[4]

The changing public agenda

We enter the 1990s in an atmosphere of growing public unease about the environment; about the public squalor which is tarnishing the increased private affluence enjoyed by many; and about widening social divisions, the most extreme manifestation of which is the return to homelessness and begging on a major scale.[5] This atmosphere makes it easier to start talking again about questions of public morality and the common good. It is encouraging too that, despite a decade 'of one of the most fearlessly ideological governments of modern times, few of its injunctions about the good and proper life appear to have impinged on the British mind'.[6]

Survey after survey has documented a stubborn adherence to the values of social responsibility rather than unbridled individual self-interest. Particularly instructive has been the annual British Social Attitudes Survey which 'shows that public opinion continues to support, in broad outline, the structure of citizenship embodied in the welfare settlement of the past four decades'.[7] However, it should be noted that the majority subscribes to a fairly limited conception of welfare citizenship and that support for more egalitarian policies cannot necessarily be assumed. The case for such policies, as essential to the achievement of genuine rights of citizenship for all, still needs to be made.

The impetus provided by closer European integration is also seen as potentially helpful to the resurrection of the ideal of social citizenship and as providing a counterbalance to the individualistic notions of citizenship emanating from the United States. The main focus of political debate here has been the 'Community Charter of Fundamental Social Rights'. However, while the Charter's recognition of the importance of the social rights of European citizens is of symbolic significance, it has very real limitations which will reduce its immediate practical significance. Some of these limitations are inherent in a Charter which is essentially about the social rights of working EC citizens and which excludes many migrant workers.[8] Others represent an (unsuccessful) attempt to make the Charter more palatable to the British Government. Nevertheless, 'whatever the speed and direction of common social legislation in the European Community, there is surely no doubt that the achievement of the internal market in 1992 will give a far sharper profile to those issues which can loosely be summed up in the expression "citizens' Europe".'[9]

The limitations of the Charter also need to be set against the less well-known European Social Charter, which, like CPAG, celebrates its 25th anniversary this year. This has been described as 'a great human rights treaty which comprehensively codifies the legal duties on the British Government to respect and advance the social and economic rights of everyone living in this country'.

A campaign for effective social citizenship could, it has been suggested, make use of this earlier Charter:

The right to work. The right to social security. The right to an adequate standard of living. The right to social and medical assistance and to social welfare facilities. The rights of people with physical and mental disabilities. The rights in this list are not just desirable social objectives. Each is a right in international law, binding on the UK government.[10]

A Charter for social citizenship

Rather than conclude with a set of specific policy recommendations, the case made in this book for the development of effective citizenship rights for all suggests a set of broad principles and policies which could form the basis of a charter for social citizenship:

1 The wages, social security and tax systems should, together, ensure that all members of society have sufficient income to enable them to meet their public and private obligations as citizens and to exercise effectively their legal, political and social rights as citizens.

To this end:

2 The social rights of all workers should be underpinned by a set of employment rights which apply equally to full- and part-time workers and which include a statutory minimum wage.

3 These employment rights should also include provisions to enable both women and men to combine paid work with caring responsibilities in the home. A first step would be to endorse and implement the Draft EEC Directive on Parental Leave and Leave for Family Reasons.

4 Access to decent jobs should be improved for groups disadvantaged in the labour market including women, black people and people with disabilities. This should include good quality training programmes, an expansion of good quality childcare facilities to cater for pre-school and school-age children; and proper support services for carers.

5 The social security system should enshrine clear rights to benefit. People should not have to depend on the vagaries of discretion or charity to meet their basic needs.

6 These basic needs should be defined in terms that provide social security beneficiaries with an income sufficient to enable them to participate in society as full citizens.

7 The social security system should be administered in a way that respects the dignity of claimants and which is more responsive to their views. Any racism in its administration must be rooted out.

8 Everyone should have equal access to and equal treatment from the social security system, regardless of race, sex, marital status, age or sexual orientation. Benefit levels should not discriminate against any one group of claimants such as the unemployed or young people. The social assistance scheme should be sufficiently flexible to take account of cultural differences.

9 The social security system should be regarded as an expression of the social rights of citizenship. To this end, reliance on means tests and contribution tests to determine elilgibility should, as far as possible, be phased out.

10 The phasing-out of means tests and contribution tests would also facilitate the provision of social security benefits on an individual basis thereby ensuring that married and cohabiting women are not excluded from the rights of social citizenship.

11 Child benefit, the 'badge of citizenship', should be preserved and significantly enhanced. The social rights of all children should be promoted by ensuring access to adequate health and childcare facilities and to an education system which does not penalise the children of poor parents by imposing hidden costs.

12 Children should not have to be separated from their parents because of poverty, homelessness or immigration laws.

13 The particular needs that people with disabilities have in exercising

their citizenship rights and responsibilities should be recognised in social security, education, employment, social service, planning and transport policies.

14 No member of society should have to be homeless because they cannot find or afford accommodation or because of inadequate 'community care' policies.

15 Taxation policies, both national and local, should be based on the principle of the individual's ability to pay.

16 Access to legal rights should not be undermined by lack of income or the unavailability of information, advice and assistance.

17 The rights of social citizenship should not be confined to those who are technically British or European citizens, but should cover all those legally resident here. Nevertheless, they should be complemented by fair and non-racist immigration and nationality laws.

A society which excludes many of its members from full citizenship puts itself at risk. Extending full citizenship rights to all is, therefore, 'the main task of social policy'.[11] As the fault-lines of inequality widen beneath our feet, this is becoming an increasingly urgent task. For the sake of the future health and stability of our society and of the 'common good' we must put an end to the divisive policies of exclusion and start rebuilding the solid foundations that an effective web of citizenship rights can provide.

REFERENCES

Introduction
1. C Mouffe, 'The civics lesson', *New Statesman & Society*, 7 October 1988.
2. S Benton, 'Claiming the fruits of the earth', *Poverty* 69, Child Poverty Action Group, Spring 1988.
3. T H Marshall, *Citizenship and Social Class*, Cambridge University Press, 1952.

Part I: The Citizenship Debate
1: The Responsibilities of Citizenship
1. D King, *The New Right: Politics, Markets and Citizenship*, Macmillan, 1987, p3.
2. J Moore, Speech to Conservative Party Conference, 12 October 1988.
3. In 'File on Four', BBC Radio 4, David Levy noted: 'The American insistence on the language of obligation rather than of entitlement has fallen on fertile soil over here,' 9 February 1988.
4. *Independent*, 14 September 1987.
5. L Mead, *Beyond Entitlement: The Social Obligations of Citizenship*, The Free Press, New York, 1986, p229.
6. *Ibid*, p257.
7. P Barclay, *Guardian*, 7 April 1988, quoted in A Digby, *British Welfare Policy: Workhouse to Workfare*, Faber & Faber, 1988.
8. J Moore, *House of Commons Hansard*, 10 January 1989, col 714.
9. See, for instance, L Burghes, *Made in the USA*, Unemployment Unit, 1987.
10. B Jordan, *The Common Good: Citizenship, Morality and Self-Interest*, Basil Blackwell, 1989.
11. L Mead, *op cit*, quoted in B Jordan, *ibid*, p82.
12. B Jordan, *op cit*, p82.
13. Archbishop of York, *Observer*, 29 May 1988.
14. Revd D Sinclair in *Dependency*, Centre for Theology and Public Issues, 1988, p7.
15. *Crossbow*, Autumn 1988.
16. B Jordan, *op cit*, p119.
17. R Dahrendorf, 'Citizenship and the modern social conflict ', in R Holme and M Elliott (eds), *The British Constitution: 1688-1988*, Macmillan, 1988, p118.
18. cf H Parker, *Instead of the Dole*, Routledge, 1989.
19. T H Marshall, *op cit*, p70.
20. W Korpi, 'Can we afford to work?', in M Bulmer, J Lewis and D Piachaud (eds), *Goals of Social Policy*, Unwin Hyman, 1989, p298.
21. R Plant, 'The fairness of workfare', *The Times*, 16 August 1988.
22. P Esam, R Good and R Middleton, *Who's to Benefit?*, Verso, 1985, p55.
23. S Allen, *Social Aspects of Citizenship*. Paper given at Queen's University, Belfast, May 1989.
24. See H Land, 'The construction of dependency', in M Bulmer, J Lewis and D Piachaud (eds), *op cit*.
25. J Brown, *Why Don't They Go to Work?: Mothers on Benefit*, SSAC/HMSO, 1989, p72.
26. L Mead and J W Wilson, 'The obligation to work and the availability of jobs: a dialogue', *Focus*, Institute for Research on Poverty, Wisconsin, Summer 1987.
27. Michael Howard and John Gummer, quoted in P Esam and C Oppenheim, *A Charge on the Community*, CPAG/LGIU, 1989, pp34 and 30.

28. S Miller, 'Thatcherism, citizenship and the poll tax', *Social Policy Review*, 1988/89, Longmans, p90.
29. P Esam and C Oppenheim, *op cit*, p143.
30. S Miller, *op cit*, p88.
31. *Ibid*, p92.
32. N Ridley, *House of Commons Hansard*, vol 131, col 581, quoted *ibid*, pp98-99.
33. F Bennett, *Poverty* 70, Summer 1988.
34. Bishop of Durham, quoted in the *Guardian*, 19 November 1988.
35. J Rogaly, 'The active citizen for all parties', *Financial Times*, 5 October 1988.
36. M Thatcher interview in *Woman's Own*, 31 October 1987.
37. D Hurd, 'Freedom will flourish where citizens accept responsibilities', *Independent*, 13 September 1989.
38. J Patten, *Guardian*, 16 September 1988.
39. D Hurd, *op cit*.
40. D Hurd, quoted in *Sunday Times*, 16 October 1988; and J Patten, quoted in *Independent*, 7 September 1989.
41. M Thatcher, *Let Our Children Grow Tall*, Centre for Policy Studies, 1977, p97, quoted in M Loney, *The Politics of Greed*, Pluto Press, 1986, p30.
42. *New Statesman & Society*, 1 September 1989.
43. C Mouffe, *op cit*.
44. A Brown, 'Cold charity that threatens to usurp the seat of justice: the limitations of active citizenship', *Independent*, 1 September 1989.
45. M Prowse, 'A new dependence on charity', *Financial Times*, 31 October 1988.
46. Bishop of Gloucester, *Guardian*, 1 June 1988.
47. J Kozol, 'Penury in the land of plenty', *Community Care*, 22 September 1988.
48. M Ignatieff, *A Just Measure of Pain*, Macmillan, 1978, p116.
49. This point was made by Sue Lieberman in 'A question of trust', *Guardian*, 29 November 1989.
50. D Anderson, *Sunday Times*, 3 December 1989.
51. R Morley, in R Cohen and M Tarpey (eds), *Single Payments: The Disappearing Safety Net*, CPAG, 1988, p65.
52. Archbishop of York, *op cit*.
53. cf T Raphael and J Roll, *Carrying the Can*, CPAG/FWA, 1984; and R Cohen and M Tarpey (eds), *op cit*.
54. cf G Craig (ed), *Your Flexible Friend?*, Social Security Consortium, 1989; and R Morley, letter to the *Guardian*, 2 December 1989.
55. F Bennett, *Poverty* 72, Spring 1989.
56. *Poverty* 1, Winter 1966, p3.
57. P Vallely, 'Justice and the market place', *Sunday Correspondent*, 29 October 1989.
58. M Brophy, *Sunday Times*, 5 November 1989.
59. cf R Lister, *The Female Citizen*, Liverpool University Press, 1989.
60. R Holman, 'Forum', *Community Care*, 24 November 1988.
61. D Hurd, *House of Commons Hansard*, 2 February 1989, col 374.
62. *New Statesman & Society*, 15 April 1988.
63. A Barnett, 'Charlie's Army', *New Statesman & Society*, 22 September 1989.
64. N Ascherson, 'Citizen put on the active list', *Observer*, 16 October 1988.
65. D Hurd, *Sunday Correspondent*, 12 November 1989.

2: The Rights of Citizenship

1. cf D Harris, *Justifying State Welfare: The New Right v The Old Left*, Basil Blackwell, 1987, p165.
2. R Dahrendorf, 'Liberty and socialism', *New Democrat*, December 1988.

3. *New Statesman & Society,* 10 June 1988.
4. *Ibid.*
5. S Hall and D Held, 'Left and rights', *Marxism Today,* June 1989.
6. *New Statesman & Society,* 10 June 1988.
7. cf M Ignatieff, 'Citizenship and moral narcissism', *Political Quarterly,* vol 60, no 1, January 1989; D Marquand, 'The subversive language of citizenship', *Guardian,* 2 January 1989.
8. J M Barbalet, *Citizenship,* Open University Press, 1988.
9 See, in particular, Raymond Plant who explores the issue of citizenship obligations from a socialist perspective in *Citizenship, Rights and Socialism,* Fabian Society, 1988.
10. R Dahrendorf, 'The erosion of citizenship and its consequences for us all', *New Statesman & Society,* 12 June 1987.
11. F Field, *Losing Out,* Blackwell, 1989, pp2, 153, 196; and see P Ashdown, *Citizens' Britain,* Fourth Estate, 1989.
12. See, for instance, J Macnicol, 'In pursuit of the underclass', *Journal of Social Policy,* vol 16, no 3, July 1987; M Bulmer, J Lewis and D Piachaud (eds), *op cit,* pt IV; *Focus,* vol 12, no 1, Spring and Summer 1989; C Oppenheim, 'Underclassed', *Social Work Today,* 26 October 1989.
13. J Macnicol, *op cit;* C Murray, 'Underclass', *Sunday Times Magazine,* 26 November 1989.
14. Dahrendorf, for instance, puts the 'underclass' at no more than 5 per cent of the population; a *New Statesman & Society* editorial (14 October 1988) equated the 'underclass' with the bottom third of society.
15. C Murray, *op cit.*
16. R Dahrendorf, 1987, *op cit.*
17. *Sunday Times,* 26 November 1989.
18. The term 'underclass' has, for example, been used freely in *The Economist, Financial Times, Sunday Times, Guardian, Observer, Sunday Correspondent.*
19. J Bradshaw and H Holmes, *Living on the Edge,* Tyneside CPAG, 1989, p138.
20. D Harris, *op cit,* p29.
21. *Sunday Times,* 26 November 1989.
22. K Thompson, *Sunday Times,* 3 December 1989.
23. R Dahrendorf, 1987, *op cit.*
24. S Hall and D Held, *op cit.*
25. F Williams, *Social Policy: A Critical Introduction,* Polity/Basil Blackwell, 1989, p206.
26. D Taylor, 'Citizenship and social power', *Critical Social Policy,* No 26, Autumn 1989, pp22 and 20.
27. cf The Sheffield Group, *The Social Economy and the Democratic State,* Lawrence & Wishart, 1989; and L Doyal and I Gough, *A Theory and Politics of Human Need,* Macmillan, forthcoming.
28. S Croft and P Beresford, 'User involvement: citizenship and social policy', *Critical Social Policy,* No 26, Autumn 1989.
29. The Sheffield Group, *op cit,* p254; M Ignatieff, *op cit;* R Plant, *op cit.*

Part II: Citizenship and Poverty
Introduction

1. T H Marshall, *op cit;* Barbalet (*op cit,* p69), however, makes a distinction between social rights of citizenship and social rights for citizenship, arguing that the latter is the valid conception.
2. B S Turner, *Citizenship and Capitalism: The Debate over Reformism,* Allen &

Unwin, 1986, p134.

3: The Civil Element

1. T H Marshall, *op cit,* p11.
2. T Lynes, Foreword, *Unequal Rights,* CPAG/London Co-operative Education Department, 1968, p6.
3. *Poverty* 10, September 1969, p2.
4. F Field, 'Establishing a free legal service for poor people'. Memorandum to Lord Chancellor's Advisory Committee on Legal Aid and Advice reproduced in *Poverty* 24, Autumn/Winter 1972.
5. T Prosser, *Test Cases for the Poor,* CPAG, 1983, p20.
6. H Rose, *Rights, Participation and Conflict,* Poverty pamphlet No 5, undated, p4.
7. *Poverty* 5, Winter 1967, p3.
8. R Brooke, *Rights in the Welfare State,* Poverty pamphlet No 4, undated, p11.
9. P Alcock, 'Why citizenship and welfare rights offer new hope for new welfare in Britain', *Critical Social Policy,* No 26, Autumn 1989, p38. See also *Welfare Rights in Social Work Education,* Central Council for Education and Training in Social Work, 1989.
10. R J Coleman, *Supplementary Benefit and the Administrative Review of Administrative Action,* undated, p3.
11. K Bell, *Tribunals in the Welfare State,* RKP, 1969, p32, quoted in R Lister, *Justice for the Claimant,* CPAG, 1974. See also J Fulbrook, *The Appellant and His Case,* CPAG, 1975.
12. K Bell, *Northern Ireland Legal Quarterly,* vol 33, no 2, 1982, pp147 and 140, quoted in M Farrelly (see note 13).
13. M Farrelly, *The Reasons Why Appellants Fail to Attend their Social Security Appeals Tribunals,* DPhil thesis, University of Birmingham, 1989, p459.
14. Quoted in the *Independent,* 5 September 1989.
15. Social Services Select Committee, *Social Security Changes implemented in April 1988,* 9th report 1988/89, HMSO, 1989, para 61.
16. F Field, 1972, *op cit,* p9.
17. Council on Tribunals, *Annual Report 1988,* quoted in the *Independent,* 18 January 1989.
18. M Partington, *The Legal Aid Means Test: Time for a Reappraisal,* CPAG, 1978.
19. Quoted in the *Independent,* 24 October 1988, and *Guardian,* 6 April 1989.
20. Eileen Pembridge, quoted in the *Guardian,* 5 April 1989.
21. G Murdock and P Golding, 'Pulling the plugs on democracy', *New Statesman & Society,* 30 June 1989; and see G Murdock, 'Poor connections: income inequality and the "information society"' in P Golding (ed), *Excluding the Poor,* CPAG, 1986.
22. See B McLaughlin, 'Rural rides', *Poverty* 63, CPAG, Spring 1986, where it is estimated from unpublished research carried out for the Department of the Environment that about 25 per cent of rural households are living in or on the margins of poverty. See also S Boseley, 'Hard times in the country', *Guardian,* 10 January 1990.
23. G Brogden, 'Welfare rights and access to information', in A Walker (ed), *Rural Poverty,* CPAG, 1978. The reference to 'The Fourth Right of Citizenship' is to a National Consumer Council report of this name published in 1977.
24. A Walker, *op cit,* p115.
25. See R Lister, *As Man and Wife?,* CPAG, undated; and R Franey, *Poor Law,* CPAG, CHAR, Claimants Defence Committee, NAPO and NCCL, 1983.
26. R Smith 'Who's fiddling? Fraud and abuse?', in S Ward (ed), *DHSS in Crisis,*

CPAG, 1985, p125.

27. For instance, evidence published by the National Association of Probation Officers, quoted in the *Independent*, 3 October 1988 and 18 December 1989; NACRO briefing paper, June 1988; Y Alibhai, 'Criminal injustice', *New Statesman & Society*, 8 July 1988.

4: The Political Element

1. T H Marshall, *op cit*, p11.
2. D S King and J Waldron, 'Citizenship, social citizenship and the defence of welfare provision, *British Journal of Political Science*, vol 18, pp425-6.
3. *Ibid*, p431.
4. M Desai, 'Drawing the line: on defining the poverty threshold', in P Golding (ed), *op cit*, p3.
5. S Ward, *ibid*, p37.
6. See R Lister, 1989, *op cit*.
7. D Piachaud, *Round About 50 Hours a Week*, CPAG, 1984, p19.
8. *Daily Telegraph*, 17 March 1988.
9. P Esam and C Oppenheim, *op cit*, p114.
10. *Independent*, 31 May 1989.
11. This point was made by Helen Kennedy at the *Marxism Today* New Times Conference, October 1989.
12. A CRE-sponsored survey, carried out by Michael leLohe of Bradford University, found almost 17 per cent of adults may be missing from the electoral register in some inner city areas, of whom about one-third gave reasons for non-registration which gave cause for concern. People of Afro-Caribbean origin formed the largest proportion of the latter group.
13. Stephen Howe, 'Dangerous apathy', *New Statesman & Society*, 11 November 1988.
14. Lord Blake, *Daily Telegraph*, 29 May 1987.
15. P Townsend, Foreword, in M McCarthy, *Campaigning for the Poor*, Croom Helm, 1986.
16. A Walker, 'Introduction: a policy for two nations', in A Walker and C Walker (eds), *The Growing Divide*, CPAG, 1987, p4.
17. *Independent*, 9 October 1989. See also *Independent*, 26 October and 31 October 1989, and *Guardian*, 15 March 1989.
18. The phrase 'infrastructure for citizenship' is taken from 'From Dependency to Citizenship', a working paper for the NCVO Study Group, 1989.
19. G Murdock and P Golding, *op cit*.
20. A Howarth, *House of Commons Hansard*, 17 October 1989, col 12.

5: The Social Element

1. T H Marshall, *op cit*, p11.
2. *Ibid*, p47.
3. R Dahrendorf in R Holme and M Elliott, *op cit*, p117.
4. D King, *op cit*, p168.
5. D Harris, *op cit*, p26.
6. M Ignatieff, *op cit*, p72.
7. D Taylor, *op cit*, p27.
8. P Alcock, *op cit*, p38.
9. The Sheffield Group, *op cit*, p252.
10. This point has been made by Jane Millar and Caroline Glendinning in 'Gender and poverty', *Journal of Social Policy*, vol 18, part 3, July 1989, p252.

11. S Hall and D Held, *op cit*. This echoes B S Turner, *op cit*.
12. G Murdock and P Golding, *op cit*.
13. D Harris, *op cit*, p149.
14. J M Barbalet, *op cit*, p44.
15. P Golding, *op cit*, p xi.
16. P Townsend, Foreword, *ibid*, pp vii and v-vi.
17. R Dahrendorf, *Inequality, Hope and Progress*, University of Liverpool Press, 1976.
18. F Bennett, *Poverty* 72, Spring 1989.
19. J Kennedy (ed), *No Mean City: A Methodist View of Poverty and Citizenship*, Methodist Church Division of Social Responsibility, 1989.
20. Report of the Archbishop of Canterbury's Commission on Urban Priority Areas: *Faith in the City*, Church House, 1985, p xv.
21. See, for instance, L Burghes, *Living from Hand to Mouth*, CPAG/FSU, 1980; V Bottomley, *Families with Low Income in London*, 1971; M Brown, 'Poor families and inflation', *Poverty* 29, Summer 1974.
22. J Bradshaw and H Holmes, *op cit*, pp138-9.
23. See E Evason, *Poverty: the facts in Northern Ireland, Ends that won't Meet*, and *On the Edge*, CPAG, 1976, 1980 and 1985.
24. D Donnison, *Supplementary Benefit and the Unemployed*. Paper given to BASW conference, 1977, quoted in R Lister and F Field, *Wasted Labour*, CPAG, 1978. See also L Burghes and R Lister, *Unemployment: Who Pays the Price?*, CPAG, 1981.
25. The physical environment, of course, also excludes people with disabilities from full participation.
26. *Poverty*, Spring 1967, p2.
27. P Townsend and D Gordon, *What is Enough? New evidence on poverty allowing the definition of a UK minimum benefit*. Paper to ISA Seminar, Edinburgh, July 1989. The figures are not strictly comparable as the 1960 figures are compiled on a household rather than an income unit basis.
28. G Murdock and P Golding, *op cit*.
29. Quoted in F Bennett, *Poverty* 73, Summer 1989.
30. S Cosgrove and D Campbell, 'Behind the wee smiles', *New Statesman & Society*, 16 December 1988. The wish to present a positive image has also been cited as a reason why some local authorities may be reluctant to embark on an anti-poverty strategy.
31. *The Bradford Revolution*, November 1988. See also Councillor M Eaton, quoted in *Community Care*, 16 February 1989.
32. See also P Dunn, 'The hungry poor fail to bounce back', *Independent*, 2 December 1989.
33. R Holme, 'All citizens now', *Samizdat*, Autumn 1988.
34. B Jordan, *Rethinking Welfare*, Basil Blackwell, 1987, p29.
35. P Gordon, *Citizenship for Some? Race and Government Policy 1979-1989*, Runnymede Trust, 1989, p3.
36. P Gordon and A Newnham, *Passport to Benefits? Racism in social security*, CPAG/ Runnymede Trust, 1985.
37. F Williams, *op cit*, p126.
38. P Gordon, *op cit*, pp7-8.
39. See *Black Claimants and the New Benefits System*, GLARE Briefing, Greater London Action for Race Equality, 1988.
40. See T Viney and G Dermody, 'Beyond the pale', *Poverty* 65, Winter 1986/7.
41. P Gordon and A Newnham, *op cit*, pp28-9 and 43. The other publication was *Double Discrimination*, published by Leicester CPAG in 1984.

42. *Ibid,* p44.
43. S Cooper, *Observations in Supplementary Benefits Offices,* 1985, p51.
44. H Arnott, 'Second-class citizens', in *The Growing Divide,* CPAG, 1987, p66.
45. K Leech and K Amin, 'A new underclass? Race, poverty and the inner city', *Poverty* 70, Summer 1988.
46. Michael Day, quoted in *Independent,* 14 June 1989, on the publication of the CRE annual report.
47. *The Responses to Racial Attack and Harassment,* Home Office, quoted in the *Guardian,* 17 May 1989.
48. N Ginsburg, 'Racial harassment policy and practice: the denial of citizenship', *Critical Social Policy,* No 26, Autumn 1989.
49. See A Hadjipateras, 'Charting the course of poverty', *Social Work Today,* 7 December 1989.
50. P Gordon, *op cit,* p26.
51. D Flynn, 'Fortress Europe – foreigners needn't apply', *Community Care Inside,* 28 September 1989.
52. J Millar and C Glendinning, *op cit,* p369.
53. See J Millar and C Glendinning, *Women and Poverty in Britain,* Wheatsheaf, 1987.
54. See G Pascall, *Social Policy: A Feminist Analysis,* Tavistock, 1986; and also R Lister, 1989, *op cit.*
55. E Abbott and K Bompas, *The Woman Citizen and Social Security,* Mrs Bompas, 1943, pp3-4, reproduced in J Clarke, A Cochrane and C Smart, *Ideologies of Welfare,* Hutchinson, 1987, pp106-7.
56. B Castle, *House of Commons Hansard,* vol 888, March 1975, col 1942, quoted in I Loach and R Lister, *Second Class Disabled,* Rights of Disabled Women, 1978, p5.
57. J Millar, 'Social security, equality and women in the UK', *Policy and Politics,* vol 17, no 4, October 1989, p316.
58. See L Luckhaus, 'Severe disablement allowance: the old dressed up as the new', *Journal of Social Welfare Law,* May 1986; and *Severe Disablement Allowance,* Disability Alliance, 1988.
59. H Land, 'Women, money and independence, *Poverty* 70, Summer 1988.
60. See C Hakim, 'Workforce restructuring, Social Insurance coverage and the black economy', *Journal of Social Policy,* vol 18, pt 4, October 1989; and J Hurstfield, *Part-timers under Pressure,* Low Pay Unit, 1987.
61. M Ignatieff, *op cit.*
62. E Meehan and G Whitting, 'Introduction', *Policy and Politics,* vol 17, no 4, October 1989.
63. For a more detailed argument see R Lister, 'Income maintenance: social security and women's poverty', in H Graham and J Popay (eds), *Women and Poverty: Exploring the Research and Policy Agenda,* Thomas Coram Research Unit/ University of Warwick, 1989.
64. R E Goodin, 'Self-reliance versus the welfare state', *Journal of Social Policy,* vol 14, pt 1, January 1985, p39.
65. J Coussins and A Coote, *op cit,* p40.
66. W Beveridge, Epilogue to the 1949 edition of E Rathbone, *The Disinherited Family,* pp269-70, quoted in S Fleming, 'Eleanor Rathbone: spokeswoman for a movement', introduction to 1986 edition, Falling Wall Press, p87.
67. M Warner, *Into the Dangerous World,* Chatto, 1989, pp4-5.
68. J Brown, *Child Benefit: Investing in the Future,* CPAG, 1988, p1.
69. cf D Hall, *Sunday Correspondent,* 19 October 1989; D Vale, *Sunday Times,*

3 December 1989; and correspondence in the *Guardian,* late 1989.

70. J Coussins and A Coote, *op cit,* p37.

71. H Parker, *op cit,* p294.

72. Save Child Benefit, *Dear Mr Moore...,* CPAG, 1988, p7.

73. *Poverty* 2, Spring 1967, p1.

74. *Income Support and 16/17 year olds,* NACAB, 1989, p22.

75. Social Services Select Committee, *Children in Care,* 2nd report 1983/4, 1984, vol 1, para 36; R Holman, *Inequality in Childcare,* CPAG, undated, updated with Family Rights Group 1980.

76. M Warner, *op cit,* p53.

77. P Townsend, 1987, *op cit,* p vi.

78. *Observer,* 12 November 1989.

79. *Observer,* 3 December 1989.

80. This case for a statutory EMA scheme was made in L Burghes and R Stagles, *No Choice at 16,* CPAG, 1983.

81. For instance, M Warner, *op cit;* A Neustatter, 'Minor problems', *New Statesman & Society,* 10 November 1989. In fact, it is reported that the UK government is unlikely to ratify the sections on immigration and nationality covering the rights of the child not to be separated from her or his parent against their will (*Observer,* 19 November 1989).

82. D Byrne, 'The rights of the child', *Poverty* 74, CPAG, Winter 1989/90.

83. D Byrne, *Guardian,* 22 November 1989.

84. Quoted in A Digby, *op cit,* pp54 and 63.

85. R Titmuss, 'The right to social security', *Unequal Rights, op cit,* p8.

86. *Into the 21st Century,* ILO, 1984, p23.

87. A Digby, *op cit,* p110.

88. J Parker, *Social Policy and Citizenship,* Macmillan, 1975, p150.

89. H Parker, *op cit,* p89. It should be noted here that the replacement of contribution by residence tests could potentially be detrimental to those not born in the UK unless the residence tests were relatively liberal.

90. cf C Hakim, *op cit.*

91. *Poverty* 5, Winter 1967.

92. R Titmuss, *op cit,* p8. However, as Hilary Rose pointed out in 'Re-reading Titmuss: the sexual division of welfare' (*Journal of Social Policy,* vol 10, p4, October 1981), Titmuss had changed his position on rights by the time he wrote 'Welfare rights, law and discretion' (*Political Quarterly,* April,1971).

93. P Corrigan, T Jones, J Lloyd and J Young, 'Citizen gains', *Marxism Today,* August 1988.

94. M Ignatieff, *op cit,* pp68-9.

95. R Titmuss, 'Social welfare and the art of giving' in B Abel-Smith and K Titmuss (eds), *The Philosophy of Welfare,* Allen & Unwin, 1987, p122.

96. B Jordan, 1987, *op cit,* p7.

97. P Taylor-Gooby, 'The future of the British Welfare State: public attitudes, citizenship and social policy under the Conservative governments of the 1980s', *European Sociological Review,* vol 4, no 1, May 1988, p18.

Conclusion: The Future of Citizenship

1. *Sunday Times, op cit.*

2. R Plant, *Citizenship, Rights and Socialism,* Fabian Society, 1988, p3.

3. B Jordan, 1989, *op cit,* p73.

4. *Ibid,* p67.

5. See, for instance, the results of a Harris Poll reported in the *Observer,* 31 December

1989, which showed that the majority believes Britain is a more divided society now than at the start of the decade.

6. H Young, 'One of us but different', *Guardian,* 8 April 1989.

7. P Taylor-Gooby, 'Citizenship and welfare', in R Jowell, S Witherspoon and L Brook (eds), *British Social Attitudes: the 1987 Report,* Gower, 1987, p15.

8. See A Hadjipateras, *op cit,* and CPAG, *Manifesto for the European Parliamentary Elections,* May 1989.

9. J Palmer, *1992 and Beyond,* EEC/HMSO, 1989, p88.

10. A Griffiths, 'In search of forgotten human rights', *Social Work Today,* 5 October 1989.

11. R Dahrendorf, 1987, *op cit.*

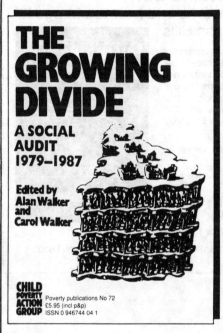

Now's the time to join CPAG!

1965-1990
CHILD POVERTY ACTION GROUP **25 YEARS** *Working against poverty*

We can help you ... with the facts on poverty.
You can help us ... in the fight against poverty.

CPAG membership gives you access to all the latest – on w
rights, income inequalities, perspectives on policy, and lots m

And CPAG members give us the support we need to ensure that
poverty is at the heart of the agenda, whatever political party is in
power.

Send off the form now, and join CPAG in our 25th anniversary year.

Please complete and send to: CPAG, 4th Floor, 1–5 Bath Street, London
EC1V 9PY.
- -
I would like to join CPAG as a comprehensive member . . . . . . ❑
(Comprehensive members receive CPAG's regular journal, *Poverty*, plus welfare
rights and social policy publications – for £35/year).

or I would like information about other membership options . . . ❑

I enclose a cheque/p.o. (made out to CPAG) for £35 . . . . ❑

Name _____

Organisation (if applicable) _____

Address _____

_____ Postcode _____